EVEN IF MY NAME WAS

JACK

I STILL WOULDN'T FIT IN THE BOX

OBATAIYE SCOTT

ISBN: 979-8-9937591-1-1 (Paperback)
ISBN: 979-8-9937591-0-4 (Ebook)

Write me at:
Obataiye Scott DOC # HQ4135
Smart Communications/PADOC
P. O. BOX 33028
St. Petersburg, FL. 33733

Email me at:
obossscott2007@gmail.com

Message me at:
Connect network.com or Connectnetwork@
AppStore: Obataiye Scott HQ4135
State: Pennsylvania
Facility: Pennsylvania Department of Corrections (DOC)

Review

I've known Taiye for a long time long enough to have watched him carry weight that would have crushed most people into silence. So when he told me he was writing a book, I didn't flinch. I just nodded, because I knew it was overdue. The world needed to hear what I'd already seen lived out in real time.

This book is not comfortable. It is not neat. It doesn't arrive with a bow on top and a safe little moral tucked inside the back cover. What it does is something far more difficult and far more valuable. It tells the truth. From the very first chapter, Obataiye pulls back a curtain most people would weld shut and walks you into the rooms where his story began. The Dirt Box. The Hate Box. The Pride Box. Every chapter is a cage he was thrown into or stumbled into on his own, and every chapter is also the story of how he broke out. Not easily. Not cleanly. But decisively.

There is a line in here that stopped me cold: "I wasn't buried. I was planted." That is the heartbeat of this entire work. Everything the world threw at him every box, every label, every whisper behind his back turned out to be fertilizer. And the man who grew out of that soil is the man I'm proud to call my brother.

As I prepare to release my own first book, I keep coming back to what Obataiye showed me through these pages: the story doesn't have to be pretty to be purposeful. Writing itself can be an act of resurrection. He went first. He kicked the door open and walked through it with his crown still on. That gave me the courage to follow.

With love, respect, and gratitude I can't fully put into words.
Your brother, always.
Walter Harris

Dedication

This book is dedicated to my late Son Clevon, who has inspired me with his smile and eagerness for life since he was a toddler. To my little Brother Jibrell, who gave of himself even when nobody knew he was doing it. To my Mother Romana C. Who taught me how to care for poor people no matter their skin tone. To my cousin Iris Rae, who always taught me that real love is unconditional. To Aunt Julia, Uncle Elick, Uncle Bern, Uncle Ron aka Dr. Bike, Aunt Marg, Gramma Gladys, Aunt Norm, Aunt Tink, Aunt Margaret, Uncle Bobby, Uncle Earl, Aunt Eleanore, Uncle Ira, Tonya Rae, Tyrone Rae, Louise, both Ruby's, Aunt Bitzy, Boo, Aunt Dianne, special dedication to my Step Pops Harry Morris and Rishan, my Amazing Father Kareim Ali with Mama Gina, no way I can forget each and every Neph that we lost in the field, and last but not least to Marzie Hattie Morgan the Great, my Grandma, who raised her kids, my Mother's kids in part and my kids. Who taught school kids for over 30 years. This one is for y'all, right out of the gate.

Foreword

We are all born into a world that places us in boxes from the very beginning. Some of those boxes come with privilege; others carry generations of pain, limitation, and expectation. Whether we realize it or not, these forces shape how we see ourselves—and what we believe is possible. My brother, Obataiye Scott, is not perfect—but none of us are. What defines a person is not the absence of mistakes, but their willingness to confront them, take responsibility, and pursue atonement. This book stands as an act of that pursuit. Life is not simple. It is layered, nuanced, and often unforgiving. We are all, in many ways, products of our environment and conditioning. But what makes this story compelling is not where it begins—it's the conscious choice to evolve beyond those beginnings. Within these pages is an honest account of a man who was thrust into an imperfect world and forced to survive. It does not shy away from truth. It does not attempt to sanitize experience. Instead, it offers something far more valuable: reflection, accountability, and the possibility of transformation. As I read this work, I was reminded that each of us carries that same potential. The journey from caterpillar to butterfly is not reserved for the fortunate or the flawless—it is available to anyone willing to do the work. Growth is not always visible. Transformation is not always graceful. But it is always possible. This book is a testament to that truth. No matter the box we find ourselves in, we are not confined to it. We can grow. We can change. And in time, we can learn to fly.

Table of Contents

It's been a lengthy journey. I've finally realized that I'm on one, too. A power trip, but not the kind you think of. It's more like a journey in a maze with hills and obstacles of all sorts.

Many of these obstacles are recurring and pop up throughout the course. Life counts, and the multitude of boxes are as far as the eye can see. It's not obvious; however, there is power to be realized and gained in this course. Hence, I say *power trip*.

Now, these boxes are synonymous with weights in a gym. We have to maneuver these boxes off and out of our way constantly or be crushed under the weight. Well, I'm sure you've heard of crazy strength or that power that wells up from within during an emergency, like saving yourself or a loved one. That power realized—it is in all of us. Surely, you know of the restructuring of the body when we rigorously train. Well, that's power gained, and the process is analogous to the circumstances in our lives, especially with so many boxes, expectations, and labels that the world expects us to fit into.

This book is for those of us who refuse to be boxed up by other folk's bright ideas and misperceptions about us that aren't really bright at all. With all these flying boxes, I had to make my way through mountains of the same. Like a cave cutter, I'm moving despite the darkness and coldness of the caves I traverse.

Many lonely highways on a journey of renewal and restoration; however, to stay back would mean to die. That box will be lowered into the ground without you or me, so let's go on this journey, sister and brother.

A journey that goes through the multitudinous boxes on the road.

THE DIRT BOX

THE TEACHER, THE TESTED, AND THE TESTIMONY

Since I can remember—my inner me has been engaged in battle after battle. So, this opening chapter is all about my testimony. Like many folks, I have keen memories that burn as they are surely wounds of great depth from those battles.

The difference today is that I'm in tune with frequencies of healing and restoration. Let the Most do what he does and heal or lie down and die.

Obataiye, don't get down like that.

Now, I know there are some folks who steer clear of good vs. evil talk, but that's what we're dealing with these days and times.

The devil would send a messenger to convey his message of sex, sickness, and hate to a three-year-old child. The first box I had to figure out was very dark, twisted, and complex. The devil is a lie, though—

since that's the message that counts. You already know who sent that one.

This box was set in the projects—70s era and its obliteration would commence almost simultaneously. The project life of old was like soul food in itself, yet sometimes the dishes it was served on were dirty.

In this situation, the dirt wasn't in the house but was very close by. A project complex back then was comparable to one big family. Usually, the closer in proximity folks lived to each other, the closer they were bonded between households. These bonds usually consisted of high trust levels and camaraderie.

We entered each other's houses unannounced and without knocking most of the time. Young parents and grandparents chastised each other's kids, and it was welcomed. We ate out of each other's pots and plates for breakfast, lunch, and dinner; sometimes, all three meals were eaten next door or across the court, or vice versa. It was not necessarily out of necessity but a kinship that didn't have to be by blood.

We cried together and laughed all the same, though. Back then, it seemed to be most good times. Unfortunately, some of these tears were brought about by contrivances of wolves that passed as sheep. In my case, the snarls and panting were disguised in a fair vibe that always included smiles and laughs. It was all subterfuge, though, and it made Houdini look novel and corny in comparison. Wolfman was pulling that wool off and using it to veil his intentions for us. I say us because the effects of child molestation devastate not only the target but the whole family, including the perpetrator's unit of the whole.

Only by the grace of the Most High was I not penetrated or killed on this battlefield. This dude's tactics should've been seen for what they were but for the blindness of fake love.

Fake affection can disarm as it was meant to; I was three years old when it started. Next-door neighbors are more like an extension of us— or so we thought. This height of hand varied and included seemingly innocent tricks like blowing smoke rings. I was intrigued, and this dude would blow these rings and get me to follow him into their house in broad daylight, yet with all that darkness lurking and formulating.

To reflect on this now, Tike is drinking vinegar. How astonishing it is to see how the father of lies works his evil machinations. The tools of his trade are more poisoned than first expected. Cancer is not the only harmful effect of all that smoke. Nobody figured he would rear his head and strike through a volley of smoke rings. Cunning, clever, and outright sneaky are just a few ways to describe this guy.

Another channel he tuned in on was my love for dogs. Their household always had a dog, and mine didn't, so this trick was inevitable due to my admiration for dogs. He made it his business to offer up his dog at every opportunity in the grand scheme. He would tell me to ask my mom and gramma if I could walk the dog with him. These walks were in wooded areas in and around our projects.

Talking about smiles that kill, right?

Thank God I didn't fit in that box either. Death couldn't hold Jesus; according to His word, He said it wouldn't hold me either.

It's profound to think about all this treachery with the clarity I now have. I could've been filled in those woods very easily by this grown man. He was young but grown.

One time, we went down under a major bridge outside the projects, where I was fondled, and he performed oral sex on me like the other times. I remember an innate alarm system going off in my soul, and I knew it was wrong, but what could I do?

I was lost in the first encounters in the beginning, but this one was different. Too many children have been tragically killed and left in the woods, just like the woods I was escorted out of by the angels spoken of in Psalms 91. Some older kids walked through and startled the Wolfman, and we left from under the bridge and walked back home in a hurry. I was definitely blessed to remember seeing the worst stories on the news. Children were being raped and murdered at a high rate. The Atlanta child murders were a big thing around the time of my situation. All of us can recall those events, I'm sure. However, the difference is that I was watching it on TV and was in danger of making news myself.

All that darkness... evil tried to bury me for sure.

News flash: On a good note, Obataiye Scott has emerged from the muck mire and dirt, emphatically....

I wasn't buried! I was planted!

The father of lies heaved a very heavy box my way, but it couldn't stop me in. The evil was no match for an angel named Ms. Crystal Wilson. Ms. Crystal Wilson was our neighbor on the other side of our house and would be as heroic as any superhero on TV.

To me, Ms. Crystal was better than Wonder Woman because she was in real life. She didn't have a truth lasso, but she was so real life and down to earth that you felt no need to lie to Ms. Crystal. In addition, Ms. Crystal would snatch you up, look you in your eyes, and say, "Now come again 'cause that ain't it." So, as best as I can recall, a few days after the bridge incident, I mentioned to Shawn, Ms. Crystal's youngest son, what was going on with this man and myself. Shawn was a few years older than me, and he was like a big bro. He was very shocked and astounded by my revelation. With no hesitation, he was pulling Ms. Crystal while calling her at the same time, "Mommy,

mommy," as we practically flew down the steps and into the kitchen where Ms. Crystal was cooking.

"Poo, tell mommy what you just told me," Shawn said in a high-pitched voice. I can still see Ms. Crystal looking down at me intensely as I spoke four words before she caught the gist and she was pulling me next door to my house in a blink. Ms. Crystal was steaming like those neck bones and greens she was cooking. My angel was insisting my mom and grandma get this dude's head on a plate. She was asking. She was mad at seemingly everybody—even at my folks. Ms. Crystal didn't play at all, and she could quite possibly be the reason I'm able to press this ink right now.

My folks called the cops while the house was in an uproar. The living room and kitchen were packed with family and friends. Everyone was asking me simultaneously. They were asking questions like: "What happened? What did he do? Are you okay?"

I remember the energy being really weird. I heard my stepdad say, "I knew something was wrong with that dude." He was speaking of the monster. My stepdad's whole thing was, "Oball, did you put your mouth on his privates?" I said, "No, he put his mouth on mine." Everybody was so upset, and the whole vibe was off as we waited for the police.

A couple of those gathered would inquire as to where the "dude" was every few minutes. I was starting to blank out into another zone because the one I was in was troubling me. By now, the police are there. I remember wondering if I was going to jail until they seemed to be on my side. They gathered with mom and grandma in a small conference off to the side. My stepdad asked if I wanted the man to go to jail or to get some help.

For some reason, I thought about Ms. Smith's love for her grandson. I also sensed that this was very uncomfortable for everyone, so I asked him to get some help. I already know what you are thinking—got damn— they left that decision up to the baby, and my answer to y'all is yes, they did.

My family and household were very close to his family, especially Ms. Smith. She was good to my siblings and me for as long as I can remember. That is until this madness was exposed. Their whole household seemed to be upset or mad at me. It was very disturbing indeed—suffice it to say we moved soon after.

To my knowledge, he began to get some counseling with no jail time. So we did them a favor by ensuring this guy's freedom and their sentiment was obvious resentment toward us.

To think back on this sort of ungratefulness, and to be fair, they were hurting. However, I can't help but notice the culprit behind the scenes and how insidious his warfare is. He does a lot of his work through some of the closest people to us. Not only do the wounds go deeper, but so does the pain when the proximity is so tangible.

I started treatment and counseling almost immediately after the smoke cleared. Western Psychiatric Institute and some other counseling was my intro to the world of mental health. The darkest one launched his best attack on a child, but I was rescued from the smoldering fire that was meant to hurt me.

There were many boxes that were, by design, supposed to metastasize and grow out of that dirt box. And so they did. I grew up out of the box instead of down into the abyss box. I have to admit, though, the complexity posed by the box set up has been quite unnerving at times. See, I got Marzie Hattie in me and Rainona C.

there, too. I've always heard their saying, "Get up boy and do your thing. Never stay down. God is in you—plus, you're a king."

These women of my life have been greatly needed and instrumental in my acquiring the maneuverability I possess. The warehouse worker gets bulky muscles from moving boxes, loading, and unloading.

Mom and grandma knew instinctively that I needed and would gain mental acuity and inner strength from the weaponized boxes that had been thrown at me. You're probably thinking of martial arts, right? You'd be wrong, although it was a dream of mine as a child to learn what the late great Bruce Lee knew. However, mom and grandma enrolled me in their love school. They shared the teaching duties and gave lessons on compassion and respect for all, especially the babies and older adults. As I grew, those lessons would, and still prove valuable.

The seriousness of sex hoisted on anyone at three years of age is heavy as it is unnatural. I surely didn't know what it was to have that type of contact—but praise God for His angels. They were with us at every lusty location.

See, I didn't know why it was happening or what it was the whole time. Psalms 91 had been applied to the scroll of my soul before I was brought on earth. My grandma knew what she was doing too. When I finally did appear in her presence, she started sowing. All those precious days and hours shared between grandma and us kids in our little project were gigantic as it relates to imparting and sowing the right seeds. Especially on Sunday, without fail, granny would fire them pots and old black skillets up. It wouldn't be complete or even normal if she wasn't playing her gospel tapes or listening to her sermons on the radio. Either way, the house was filled.

This was one of the grandma's ways of pleading Jesus's blood over us and into our lives. If we even acted like we wanted to snap a finger to jam as if this was secular music, grandma would tap our bottom. She had to give us that look most of the time and say, "No, you don't." We'd straighten right up and maybe even just go ahead and sit down. She had no problem sending me outside to strangely get my own pain relief. You guessed it—yeah, some fruits off the bush—and I brought them back directly, as grandma would almost spell out.

I didn't understand it in my child's mind, but innately, I was inspired by the reverence of the occasion of grandma's worship. She was the light post that directed the angels to the dark dungeon. Ms. Crystal and Shawn would be the first to descend onto the big block stone dungeon door. It took the strength of both of them to open the door—it was so heavy and squeaked as it opened. The door itself was a box of the worst kind. This is exactly why its obliteration was a must.

At this time, nothing else matters but the annihilation of every false belief we've sent forth. Many of these beliefs start early in life; ideally, we want and expect positivity, encouragement, and reverence for Good to be cultivated in the house. Clearly, these principles are fortifying to all persons blessed to receive them. The process for my fortification was tainted behind that heavy, ugly, dark door. Anger took root in me—yes, even at that early age. Friends of the family would always comment that I was so handsome but so evil too. When I heard that, I didn't know if I should be flattered or if I was just evil. If they all only knew—including mom and gram—why I was so mad, too. These cute moments I spoke of were before the curtain was pulled back on this guy's dark room.

I poignantly remember feeling angry and having a bad attitude as a child. I felt like a little man with the same weight or more on my shoulders than any patriarch. Now, I knew what that was or meant at the time, but y'all know where I'm at it. As the years came and went, mom's team grew, and I was the eldest. As I had the first birthright, I would also have the honors of big bro, and responsibilities came with the honors. Big brother syndrome came with symptoms of business. Whenever the abuse I suffered reared its ugly face, I was surrounded with love and care from my mom and grandma—the damage incurred from the abuse was hit with a massive counterblow. Mom and grandma made sure to instill in me all the reinforcements I could handle. Thanks to them and my Lord and Savior Jesus

Christ. I decided early on that Obataiye was a winner, and even though I was molested, I was glad to be a life participant.

Now, to be fair to my dad, he also inculcated the key concepts and precepts in me. He gave me my first lesson on sowing and reaping. I was probably two when we lived in a house on Kelly Street in Homewood. My dad enjoyed growing vegetables, and he would have us in the garden with him, giving me the steps one by one.

He wasn't around long, as my parents got divorced almost as fast as they were married, I guess. I would say, though, that he always reminded me to take care of my room and sisters. And after he chipped in where he could, he and my mother would always define my name very profoundly, explaining that Obataiye meant king of the world. So I just shipped right over the prince stage and went straight to the king status. And I was the eldest sibling. You couldn't tell me anything. I was in my kingdom, and that's just that, so I carried myself as such. There was undeniably a facet of my attitude that was off-putting at times, especially to my family. Unbeknownst to me, that unpleasantness mentioned above occasionally reared its head; however, disruption is a prerequisite of growth, and it was God's plan to grow me through it all. Even the soil that I was surrounded by was disrupted by my growth. In fact, disruption indicates growth.

The sky is only an observation area—not the limit, as so commonly stated. Surely, there was a transmutation taking place, a changing of positions of my confusion and anger into perseverance. I didn't know exactly what was taking place, but I always remembered my faith inwardly in the Most High, not to mention my folks taught me about my king's blood.

Dignity over pride is a concept I had to eventually grow into and through.

Mom, grandma, dad, and even a few others were early guardians who would ensure the dignity lane was the most traveled. The lane still meanders, winds, and dips down into the dirt box.

Those king's teachings and nerve assertions registered in my soul that I wouldn't fit in anybody's box, even if my name was Jack. Facts be told that my folks' edification of me do not limit what the Most High had placed in me before I was born. See, all that early nurturing enabled me to deal with the weight of all the other boxes I would soon have to endure. Not only to endure but to figure out who I am in relation to those boxes and misnomers.

Some were heaved a t me, and admittedly, some I walked into out of my own volition. In fact, in 2019—the year of Covid—not only did Covid strike, but so did a part of my earliest plight in life.

I lost My way and chose the company of two different people in the LGBTQ community. This period preceding my choice was a very dark period and I hit the default button. Yes, something that caused so much pain and disturbance throughout the life I chose now to explore. Things went hay way almost immediately. The first one looked very similar to a biracial female. The look drew me in. The long hair and ponytail proved to be a mirage. Everybody in the jail that was in the LGBTQ lane was after this guy. He had just gotten to the jail, and it was obvious he was new to the prison thing on the whole due to his young age. He was in his twenties, so yeah, it got crazy. They were choosing... and he was too. From my observation, that's a very promiscuous lane. I didn't sign up for all that ensued.

For one, this was my second bit upstate, and being so far into my second bit to have this type of breakdown shocked the world and me. That surprise definitely sent out shock waves due to surprise. The hate that already existed toward me exploded. Most of it was hypocritical, too. Most of the backbiting and whispering was being partaken by those who indulged in that lifestyle themselves or condoned it and ignored it when it involved their tomboy or someone they feared. It's all a dimension of the dirt box, though—little did they know—so is the ascension, and Taiye was equipped with Psalm 91.

I believe that scripture was brought into my life unbeknownst to me, specifically 91:11-12: "For He shall give his angels charge over you, to keep you in all your ways. In their hands, they shall bear you up, lest you dash your foot on a stone."

I could've caught AIDS had I gone there, but again, God kept me. There are known AIDS carriers in that zone. That would've been a helluva, but by God's grace kept me. It's a deep thing to really experience my Higher Power and his angels drive when I was seemingly destined to crash.

On the flip side, due to the invigoration of my soul, I now know that my mistakes don't define me. If anything, they help to find me. It was a defining moment as surely, I learned who I'm not.

I had to do some serious digging akin to unearthing massive dirt during this time and subsequent climb. It truly felt like I was buried even when that still, small voice said, "Obataiye, you were planted... not buried." That's when I discovered that the dirt thrown on me was loaded with fertilizer.

Many burned rubbers, leaving the realm of what I thought was a friendship or even kin. But Troy—aka HEA, stayed and even said to me: "Hey, Ob, don't even sweat it, dawg. That's just the fat burning off." That was profound.

That's the only word I can use to describe the feeling when he said that. We agreed on how so many folks with false principles do things that they point and whisper about. This is the dirt box state! The same dirt they throw is the same dirt they're buried in.

So many people condone, excuse, or participate secretly—or overtly—yet have so much to whisper about and say. Jesus said, "Let he who is without sin cast the first stone." Everyone in attendance just started dropping their stones and walked away. Jesus could have cast His, but he didn't. He held back out of mercy and compassion.

There was no condemnation from the Son of Man. God in the flesh stooped with the lowest of the low to pick them up. He didn't come for the false high and thought to be mighty. And that goes for me too. No condemnation from me or looking down on the LGBTQ community; however, many from that community attempted to look down on me. All because I chose the lifestyle I wanted. You leave to give; thanks, Troy, for sticking around.

I didn't even associate much with members of that community except for the two I chose. People are truly lost if they feel you owe them some type of conversation because you feel how you feel. It is disrespectful to even think like that. Again, thanks Troy, for the respect that you demand. Respect is paramount and should be reciprocated.

I chose not to be involved in that lane or lifestyle, period. You waste time hating me for my choice, but still, it would be better to concentrate efforts on your ventures in life. There's a deep freedom in letting go and letting God take control. Let go, mate; let go of the self-condemnation and the projections of negativity. Therein lies progress and self-improvement.

Some people have expectation boxes, but sorry, I'm not fitting in anybody's box. Even if my name was Jack, flipside—I was creating to exceed expectations, not meet them, get out of the car and settle there.

Yes, I was tainted—wounded in my childhood, and those scars are proof of healing. It's an honor to wear them, and I wouldn't trade them in for the world. God chose me in these scars. In fact, He chose me in the wounds before the womb. So yeah, I'm tapping into this divine hand that created and now guides mc. This is a true high and the loudest Hallelujah—1've been through a lot to get it.

I must admit that it was surreal and painful in that disruption to my peace. To be judged and talked about by closet gay dudes whom I'd seen with my own eyes sneaking in and out of moon homosexual's cells. All the years before and during my tribulation, to think of the audacity and fakery of the caliber of so many is, to this day, mind-blowing. But I convert the angry steam into energy to stay on top and ahead of the ever-so-coining lot. I emerge in front of the dirt, yet my roots are there, running deeper than the scars. Today, I'm well nourished, and through Christ, I am growing and becoming more than a conqueror. I'm not mad because a few people were calling me Big O. The very thought is minuscule. That was a box. I'm not Jack in that.

I could've chosen to spiral out of control and stab, rant, rave, busting dudes in the head. It was tempting, and I was hurting, honestly—but that still small voice said, "Obataiye, why try and protect the illusions of a psycho pathetic killer?" Thai's not who you are, beloved. That's dead, and you were raised with Christ's resurrection, and not even the vicissitudes and effects of child abuse could withstand that power that holds us up today. Not hatred, jealousy, envy, self-hate, false pride, vanity; none of that. Revenge, immoral sex, pornography, smug abuse; all that was nailed to the stake with the cross on Calvary.

Perseverance at its best was transferred to Him. He looked up and said in a loud voice, "It is finished." And because of His finished mission, I can forgive. Forgiveness I give to all because it's not box-worthy. By grace, we all can receive it if we give it. Besides that, I'd be remiss not to utilize some of the best gifts around. Why hold it in the form of resentment when we can transform it into fuel by forgiving? It's plentiful and cheap, yet potent enough to propel rockets blasting through dirt boxes.

All this muck and mire on these lower levels definitely opens eyes or causes folks to close them permanently. I'm opting to grow and go even in the cold. It was quite disheartening in the dirt box—and it was levels to it. I was planted well below the top soil. I was being hated by the people I taught in the school. They tried to knock me at my lowest point. Bunch of Judas was my constant thought, daily and nightly. Even in my sleep, it felt like the world was caving in on me.

There are some people you expect to sell you out, but others you'd swear up and down they were like your siblings. It hurt so bad I had to laugh so I didn't cry; lo and behold, I really started laughing. After the scales fell off my eyes, I realized that many wanted to be me while speaking and faking salutation. Fake, well, it's all in these Pure Dirt.

I've been well off in these jails as it relates to money-end basics. I'm not bragging, but the significance lies in the jealousy aspect of it all. The eyes are the windows, and even when they overly complimented me on some fifty-dollar commissary shoes, I saw straight through them. Dirty windows, I guess you can say it, right? This is what it is in those boxes, and that's why I never fit in and never will.

Before and after these particular trials and tribulations, I didn't and still don't let anybody get too close. I've always picked and chosen even my patrons. This part of my character burned folks up, too. People feel like, who does he think he is that he ain't get to deal with me? Instead of just keeping it pushing, they stew in resentments that give off a smell. Stinky stew, too. It's the kind that starts smelling when trials befall a guy and it senses you down. Attempts on my character, however, I've come to reflect and realize that my futile character is too fibrous and real to die. Reputation, well, that's taken some hits, admittedly, but I'd sacrifice my reputation to know what I know now.

Furthermore, my faith aligned with Romans 5:3-4, and not only that, but "But we also glory in tribulations, knowing that tribulation produces perseverance, and perseverance character, and character, hope." It doesn't get any realer than that. It's all about this restoration now as I go deep inside myself to connect with the Most High. I was so moved by my inner self and I decided that I was and could never be destroyed by something I have authority over. A whole lot of evil in that realm I was fooling with. It seemed to onlookers that the odds were stacked against me again.

Believe me, I felt like they were, too. I was trained there, though, in my younger years. Now the bettors sweat as their losses creep up on them from the recesses of their mental makeup. The difference with me is that I remember others - no matter who - who are struggling in prayer. All that backstabbing had me stumbling as it was surely delivered blow by blow. But then again, one can get a cobra to appear by throwing some pennies in the air. Dirt box.

My whole thing is to take off like a rocket, and it has been since way back. To lift off is to leave all the negative energy to stack amongst its likeness. There's so much going on in those lower levels that many won't make it back up. The weight on the shoulders, back, legs, and heart is literally too physical—from the unseen to the seen.

This is why my weapons are spiritual. It's bigger than the flesh. Those who've been through a thing or two know just what I'm talking about. In the dirt box, its serpents are worse than cobras. To use a physical sword would be an endless losing undertaking. See, I like to win; in fact, I love to win in life. But I had to get up first. Who's better to have in your corner was a question playing in my mind's eye. Then, dazed, I looked over to my corner, and in all that glory, He said I AM.

I've been moving ever since the vital realization that He in me is greater than He in this world. It's a different vibe. It's a war out there; sometimes, mental battles within the self occur. But overall, the inflow I tap into now is divine and uplifting for certain. I'm investing no time into nobody's boxes: gossip, slander, none of that. That's weird to me especially since those weapons were aimed at me. But lo and behold, no weapons formed against me shall prosper. Hallelujah, I've learned a lot in the trenches of life right up through now and as a pupil. I'm taking heed.

One hard lesson, but understood and appreciated, is that there could be no wins without suffering losses. Muscles grow only after being torn down by way of many burns. I could hear my forefathers and mothers of old saying, "Let the impurities burn out, son. It gets greater later." Granma Marzie Hattie is in my ear saying, "Oball, dust yourself off, baby, and go in to win now. You are a winner, Oball, and always have been." As I drop salt water out of my eyes, I look up and tell my Grandma, "I hear you, Granma, and now they have to deal with me." I give thanks today for who and what I've become through it all.

See, my battles, as has yours, consisted of eliminating the boxes by tapping into frequencies other than the bull crap. But all in all, what they say about crap being good fertilizer is true. Now I welcome the stench—I just recharge on reminders of angels of God.

Positive growth spirals up, and the roots are fortified with nutrients in the dirt. The darkness we endure can be purposeful, but we should not see it as such. I'm done taking the tows so personally. I can't stay down for long without figuring it all.

My best gills were discovered shockingly in the dirt—in the pain, muck, and mire. On my worst day, I was uplifted to shine through the hate, causing some of it to turn into its opposite. The day is new, the proper adjustments have been made, and there's more to come.

The effort, most definitely, must be persisted upon like a jackhammer on a construction site. Now, the distinction is sharp between a jackhammer and a Jack in the box.

Student: Teacher, what shall I do with this dirt?

Teacher: Appropriate it—that box is in your mind, not mine. Student: No wonder I don't fit in it.

THE HATE BOX

CAN SOMETHING DIVIDED STILL FIT IN A BOX?

Let's walk while we talk about this next box. The motion of our gait will surely prevent its landing on us. This one is tricky, too, because the materials of this box often stack within us.

It's simple but damaging, end complex at the same time. HATE.

It is so destructive when misappropriated. I say that because to hate, certain things are needed to shame them off of us. Vices of any kind—where I'm concerned, I not only hated but I despised. They had to go one by one over the years, going way back to the 90s. I hated being on drugs, slowly and sometimes quickly melting away my life. Eventually, the hate I felt toward being a loser caused me to recalibrate and tighten up the mental screws and bolts. One of my constant thoughts was: "I'm not going out like this."

At this time, I was in my early to mid-twenties, and the healthy hate fostered an attitude alert within me. So yeah—without a doubt, there needs to exist a healthy hate for what can cause us to be unhealthy.

On the flipside, there is spitefulness, pettiness, ugliness, and quite frankly, disgusting type of hate. This type is synonymous with jealousy, envy, condemnation, judgment, and even self-loathing.

Self-loathing because, ultimately, to be so hateful is essentially hate for oneself. Self-hate sometimes causes one to project their inner conflict onto unwitting folks who are just being themselves and mingling with their own business.

Bad energy is the driving force behind most, if not all, the killings and enemy incidents we're witnessing and experiencing. This box is definitely a bad habit that must be broken. Unhealthy hate is a bad habit by nature and is pure negativity. Yes, its drawing power is deceitful because we don't admit it when we're under its influence. However, it can and must be broken. Once it's broken, it's time to get up and take flight.

Boxes can strangely but surely have a drawing power to them because we feel comfortable in them. These comfort zones are tricky because their end is darkness. All the chit-chat and bickering while we smoke and indulge in other vices akin to what guardrail is to the basement; it's hypocrisy. These days, it's all about the self-reprimand and moving steadily within our inner guardrails. Example story:

I'm not settling for anything less than conceive, believe, and retrieve.

The devil has been sending them at me since my birth until today. I've faced hate day after day for many years in these jails just for being me. I always handled my needs even when there was very little to no money. I ran little petty in-cell stores, yet the hate they generated—you would think—I was selling hate pills.

To make it worse on the envious, networking and mingling gracefully is natural for me. I never joined issues into the geographical box among the cell mates or neighborhood squabble. Nor did I separate myself by city. I'm known from all corners, and I recognize the grace in others as well.

This attitude has always garnered swaths of admiration and alliances over the years. However, you know, when we do that, we can't just let any and everybody get too close, especially when we observe snake-like acts from short or long distances. It's crazy because people truly are oblivious to the fact that some of us do pay attention to our surroundings and the actions of those in them. So when we put up barriers, that further infuriates the mate in these bystanders. Now, hold up; let me tie this into the whole scenario.

Fast forward to 2019—the two situations we discussed earlier. I put myself in the lane of the LGBTQ community. It's 2023, and the devil still got the masses chewing on the old cud. This is no surprise. It's protocol—I know. And I stand firm still crowned-up Obataiye. The scandal box had levels that went deeper, exposing more hate and fakeness than I originally thought was there. Folks who prophesied their love one minute did the opposite the next. Even some on the streets allowed their ears to be bent by wickedness. A lot of the circulating was false and a lot of folks knew that but would rather continue with the lies too.

Lo and behold, it started to be revealed to me that there also exist levels of fake love too. With these revelations from the Most High, it was only applicable for me to love myself in deeper ways than ever before. I experienced and still see through fake well-wishing and smites straight to the hate behind the windows to the souls. I have no choice but to love me, and love me I will do.

There's a lot of pain in the delivery room of life, but the pain gives way to understanding and better living than before. All in all, it was my choice after those situations in that community for me to be heterosexual, especially due to my faith as a Christian.

I do salute the LGBTQ community, though. Y'all are some very brave and courageous people well within your rights to exercise your will. Free will is a Goal. And no one has the right to judge another, especially when their closets are of the walk-in sizes.

It's been some years since my stint in that lane, yet I still get the weird fake looks. I don't regret my experience because it exposed a lot to me as it relates to folks' true nature. Had I chosen to live within that lifestyle or not, the hate always existed before I did what I did. That was just an excuse to openly castigate me in the first place.

Remember my dawg HEAD? When he said to me, "...that's just the fat burning off... let them go."

These days, I deeply desire to keep on keeping on and over-standing and overcoming mediocrity and downfalls, so I move accordingly. Way too many people are praying for my demise, not knowing they add fuel to my rise every time I see my reflection in their hateful eyes. To be caught up in a box is akin to death. This is largely why I began to focus intently on transcendence. Yes, it's easily spoken, but keep in mind that speaking and believing precede achievements.

It's deep when we peer into a mere idea of folks' desire for others to adhere to their devices, a.k.a. little boxes.

As I write these words, it dawns on me that the Most High extended His sustenance and subsistence to me. I feel and think this is transformational as it relates to overcoming these traits.

There's no way in the world that I can fold myself up to fit in anyone's box after the real edition of who I am in God and who I'm not. How beautiful it is to ascend from the depths after diving so deep into the muck and mire of delusional thinking. It's literally delusional to even imagine that we are less than as opposed to being greater than. This is when 1 John 4:4 says, "Little children, you are from God and have overcome them, for greater than he who is in the world."

As I nod, I say hmmmmm....

It's deep how when I traversed this compound, it conveyed via the aura and the ether how many wanted to kill my spirit. They still hope in vain that my journey takes me out. I see in their glance the disappointment that the potholes and rough weather only steadied my crown and polished it. As I look back at them, I tip my crown to them, and in my prayer time, I pray for the forgiveness of their sins and for love and healing to abound in their lives. See, little do most know that to fit in a box is to tip over a rod and die. The college of thought I attend is of infinite—eternal life, which is the gift of the Most high. For many years, I strove to fit into boxes and expectations of others. Even though I wasn't good at it, I never realized my errant ways. I've spent many years stressing out, trying to please and come through for so many, and I abandoned my principles in the process. A lot of that striving on my mat was me feeling like I should level down so as to melt the envy I caused in folks.

In reality, we could never make everyone around us happy, especially in terms of our sanity and wellness. We leave our very own scruples unattended when we get lost in Boxville, PA.

These days, I believe there is power in being centered, goat-oriented, and with sortie healthy optimism, along with being filled with faith. Being boxed up down on their shelves of inadequacy, pettiness, and delusional thinking is unacceptable. Drug dealer, been there done that... gangster, been there done that... penny army thistle, been there too... player all the way to high school, dropped out and bragged about it. It's no surprise that I failed, but somehow, in that box, I didn't expect to pass, though. Those are the decisions I'm talking about.

All these boxes, bruises, and scars just to mingle at a hate-filled party. Not to mention the mass shootings and the correlations to this hate box we're discussing. For me, I'm not resorting to violence, even in the face of all this debauchery and ill feelings. That's the easy way out. I'd rather go through what I'm going through to get to where I'm going.

At some point, the obvious choice we all have is to level up off of the shelves. Recognizing us, we take to activism and embody our part and access to the universal storehouse. It's our God-given right to reach and stretch past even our own earliest expectations of ourselves.

Will follicles feathers get ruffled? Probably, but hopefully, when they stop hating, they straighten up and fry right, too. Feather ruffling is a regular occurrence in crows when they encounter the broadness in the wingspan of the bald eagle-pun intended. All you other eagles fly high, too. You know, I see y'all too if I can spot a mole hiding in a field or face full of diversionary smiles—I definitely see y'all in all y'all greatness.

As I reflect, observe, and analyze people's reactions and actions in response to what I do, this anomaly tremendously effectuates an alert within me. Any time you do something as simple as tying your shoe and folks watch and then converse about your shoes—you're approaching Triumphant breakthrough, or maybe you are there? Surely, some watch in admiration, but it is also true that some watch with despicable notions.

Indeed, the eyes are the windows to the soul. It took a while to figure this out, but I got these. I believe the revelation had a great deal to do with the cup I was sipping from. You know those false cups of hidden malice, which is poison in itself. When I drank from the false friend cup, I saw the lower region of my face. When I drank from the hunter's cup, this cup was larger, and I saw my whole face in the reflection of the bottom of the cup.

While drinking from the cup of fake well-wishers, I saw the bridge of my nose and had an epiphany. I merged with the perseverance in me and decided I'in on my way across this bridge. I'm not knocking down any more bridges except the ones I extended to dream killers.

This next cup I drank from, I saw my eyes and the crown of my head; however, this one is from God, and surely it runneth over. I heated my big cousin Iris in icy soul saying: "Baby, you've got to go through it to get to it."

To spend too much time in Distraught Ville, PA, is to lose in life, and that's not an option. How are they going to blackball Oball?

They can't!

Losing is never in our plans, but if we're not mindful, others will fail. Envision how truly massive this world is—now picture how small a box is in its efforts to end constant outward projection onto others in vain. You'd think with all these shenanigans from the depths, I'd be on edge with anger. On the contrary, I'm at peace.

For me to remain resentful and flame at one or two is already more than enough. Life is massive and precious—too precious to waste on waste. To focus on folks' downfalls or stumbles is proof of the beholder's low level of living and thinking.

In all reality, brothers and sisters, there are some truly amazing goals to be made. Winners have goals even after earlier victories in life. You know, even the small ones are wins. When you quit smoking—victory—when you saved up and started that business—victory—when you raised the babies to fear God and stay in school, guess what, another victory. That's big time! When you put drugs down and choose to stack your money. Goals, right?

Now, on the flipside, there are surely goalies playing defense. You better believe hate is in bold letters on their game-day jerseys. They were exercising for this, and that's okay because we exercise as we go these days. We have to be persistent through the mud, muck, and mire, knowing it won't last. That's how we maintained all those prior victories—being consistent with the principles such as never giving up, being true to ourselves, respecting all but fearing none, having compassion for our fellow human beings, and being doormats for no one, to name a few.

To all my x-felons, to get out of jail and survive all the way in a lane going the opposite direction is likened to driving against the traffic of a very busy road.

Sure to crash burn to a crisp! My whole thing is self-mastery. It's a must. One thing about being bombarded by all those boxes is that I gained fortitude. This fortitude was cultivated in the darkest of times. Some and most of the roads were more like trenches that meandered sharply. Lo and behold, though, because I see how that self-mastery steadies the way. Tapping into this divine inner-self instilled by no other than the Most High is my go-to. Activism and nothing less these days. The two-level impulse feeding really gets to be detrimental to our higher plans, knowing full and well that our babies, siblings, younger cousins, nieces, and nephews all need and expect optimal results from us.

It should be shameful to get all jammed up in a compactor full of mate boxes. That's exactly where that road leads. I don't want any parts or pieces. The way I see it is that it's time to live off y'all. Even in these bars, I'm in a place mentally and spiritually where I can't lose. My attitude is one of a deteriorative nature. I've hit the bottom—rock bottoms, and it hurts eight days a week, twenty-seven hours a day. Even in a fallen state, I was talked about like a dog and looked at like I stole their refrigerator out of their house on Thanksgiving Day. Little did they know that they were helping me mature.

At times, I sat on the edge of the steel slab of a mattress. The weight on my soul would struggle to push me toward the floor as I sat there looking at the TV. I would laugh at times as it felt like I was being stabbed in my soul.

You heard me, right?

It hurt so bad that I would laugh. I wasn't numb, or it wouldn't have hurt. I was in an immense recalibration mode. Muscles were being formed on the inside as well as the outside. The hate was the weights I trained with.

Thank you!

See, this is why I have to praise God. Let me expound on that for a minute.

It was the early 80s upper Hill district, Morgan Street, to be exact. Summertime in the Burgh, and the sun was setting beautifully to cap a nice long day of hoping and toying with honing little rap skills. My homeboy Fat Dave, a.k.a., Bundy was geeked up to let me hear his new Fat Boys album hot off the presses.

So we trekked to his crib on ole Morgan from the hoop court on Wandless Hill. It was something about this day and particularly this interval. There was a certain lightness to it. Thinking back, in part, Big Bundy felt a special lightness in spite of his size. The Fat Boys were the hottest thing out on the air waves.

Everybody was talking about Buff, the human beat box, and those mean beats he was spitting out. Overall, all three of the Fat Boys were just as smooth as they wanted to be. And all that smoothness they conveyed to my friend Dave that being fat wasn't a hindrance but an advantage. That same lightness was conveyed as it emanated from my bro to me.

As we set up in his room, listening to this new crew going in on the wax, I was amazed at the sounds, especially Buff's beat boxing. Immediately, I started trying to imitate the sounds of Buff's prolific beats. It was birdied in me right then and there. One of my earlier goals started to take shape in my mind's eye.

After we both excitedly listened to the new album and tried to imitate the Fat Boys, we decided to go outside. Down the steps we went—Dave's mom and dad lovingly engaged us in light greetings, and that classical, "Y'all boys be good," and "okay mom, alaight dad," Dave said, and out the door we went. As we headed out the front yard, a friend of Dave's parents was on his way past us. He was a dapper gentleman in his sixties. I remember always seeing Dapper Dan in the neighborhood. He was always walking, and sometimes seemed to be whistling and just as serene as possible. He had the little top hat, dress slacks, and a short-sleeved shirt. Add to that his two gold chains, watch, and rings. The whole shebang! Dapper Dan was that dude y'all.

As we strolled toward him, he stopped us with a greeting, "What's up little brothers, y'all rollin'? Strong man, stay like that now, you hear me? Say, let me ask you something."

Dave said, "what's up, unc?" and then I added, "yeah, what's up unc?" Dapper Dan smiled. "Do y'all know what perseverance means?"

We looked at him like dogs look at the TV when they tilt their head in confusion. Then we looked at each other and said in unison,

"Nahhhhh." Then, the lesson of an angel began. Dapper Dan grabbed out attention with an authenticity that still shines through today. He told us that to persevere meant never giving up in life. To keep on going in the roughest times no matter how bleak things look. He would restate the word throughout his soliloquy, but for some reason, it didn't tire us out or run us away. It was something in his message to us boys that was meant for us to receive. He delivered this idea, this gilt, this jewel to us with urgency, but again, strangely, it was easily palatable.

A lot of times, folks ran youngins into closed ear hall with their drunk or highly hypocritical speech. This was different, and to this day, I remember and cherish this jewel called perseverance. I don't know where Big Bundy is today, but I hope and pray he kept and used his jewel, too. After Dapper Dan schooled us, he shook our hands like we stood as tall as him. He smiled, tipped his hat to us, and said, "Aaight now, perseverance y'all," before turning away and walking and whistling a fine tune.

Dave and I continued discussing the word in astonishment at Dapper Dan's class on the walkway. Let it be no wonder that I named my only daughter, *Endure*, years later. Almost immediately after that lesson on rare life, I sent baby roots down into the case of the up-and-coming hip-hop culture arid scene. Although I started out rapping, I had my inner ear honing in on them beatbox techniques.

I started writing and memorizing my raps, spitting them to the imaginary sold-out crowd in the bathroom mirror at 706 Webster Terrace across from the old fire station. At this time, I was going to Prospect Middle School in Pittsburgh's Mt. Washington neighborhood, overlooking all three rivers. All of us would be gathered in the cafeteria upon arrival at school. This was every morning of the week. Naturally to us, with this hip-hop thing in full swing, you had your best beatboxers engaged in some of the first —spittin' an all—back and forth in high pandemonium fashion. I mean, with all the prospects, the cafeteria seats would soon be filled again at lunch time. Rap battles and just us kids honing in on our new found lore called hip-hop.

Every now and then, someone might snap out on the drum set that was up on the stage in the cut. I mean, you can't make this stuff up. Everybody rocking in sync, "Ohhhhhh! Ohhhhhh! Ohhhhhh!" to the heat early in the morning until we were given our direction for the day by the guidance counselor and teachers who were never far away. So one morning, in this meeting of young geniuses in the making, I met Wesley Smith, an up-and-coming rapper in the Hill District and in school. We were sitting at the same table in the cafeteria, and he was working on a new rap, as was I. We put our skills on display—reading right off the page for the crows in our immediate space. The rest is history. Wes and I became the best of friends and started writing raps in tune with each other, like Run DMC and EPMD.

We could go back and forth and just flow for mini concerts on site. You couldn't tell us anything. In no time, flat one was beatboxing exclusively. I started with the blu to glu the beat my homeboy *Cripple Doug Braxton* helped me master.

Not to be cruel, but that's just how it was in the hood nickname vernacular. We loved Doug like a brother. That beat helped me form for myself, spawned and metastasized into a monster beat eventually through the city. I got deeper and deeper into the beat game, and I basically stopped writing raps. Beat boxing was my gift, and I gave off my gift while Wes Luv rapped. We performed and turned out school talent shows with his surgical rhymes and my blu to glu that everybody was talking about. The boy Oba and blu to glu. It was pandemonium. So much lore and passion for life that there was no room for hate. It tried to poke its nose in our movement from time to time in the form of a jealous, less talented striver.

I just told them to stay calm and collected and to persevere like me. Overall, that hate box was out of place in our ranks back then. It was too much camaraderie and fun. It couldn't fit over all of us. Simply too small—this hate box was. It's still too small when we embody the truth, which is love. The frequency, the reality, and the cure for all ailments, physical, mental, and spiritual. It took the crack monster to roar into the veins of our communities. The way I see it is exactly that. The hate wasn't enough by itself, so it went and got reinforcements.

The term player-hater wasn't even in existence or thought about until the monster yelled out at us. Without acknowledging the concept of divide and conquer, it's hard to understand most of our plights. That's the drug box that lies in the rudimentary level of a lot of the hate we're enduring right now. The detainee box is another box, but its correlation is evident in the hate. They go hand in hand, and they're holding hands but not out of love. We'll go deeper into the discussion on this box a little later. That's a heavy box, and the perseverance works mentioned above wonders on it, as well as this dark sentiment right here, right now. It's way far superior and past hate to be a person of positive change than to be one of the bunch. Sometimes, it might take us to glance back to more innocent tribes to get back in tune with love, beats, or whatever is going on in your life.

We find ourselves earnestly delving into who we were before all the competing and realized that the best versions of us still exist. The taint of the crack era bred a different type of competition. It does offer an excuse for many of the hateful and petty characteristics embodied by many. All of it too! Me included.

I admit my part in the cycle of always competing with the folks around me. It generates a very obvious horrible energy that's undeniable. Once I realized how far I strayed from truly living, laughing, and loving, I decided enough was enough. It's entirely too much invested in unspoken, low-key competition between us. That's envy and jealousy at play. I'm in races that are unbeknownst to me more than half the time. Then it becomes obvious when I see myself being literally mirrored. To make it worse, it's always someone who slipped up and let me in on their true sentiment of envy toward me. Then, in true form and definition of a paradox, mimic my every move. Whether it be a business strategy, a particular way, an idea, or a concept I shared with them or they observed. They'd literally improve on it and make the tone to inspire people—but have the decency and integrity to acknowledge who inspired you. Don't hate on me. Actively work against me, slandering and backbiting the whole time, knowing I gave you my basics that are now your primary embodiment. It's preposterous!

What's he got? How much? 1 can do better than him—who does he think he is? These are the thoughts and words that were constantly rotating in the immediate ether.

Where's the camaraderie?

It's mostly jealousy and envy, and in jail, that's really pitiful because these are commissary shoes and sweats. Chips, cakes, and e-cigarettes with some noodles on the side y'all. Please! There's nothing to it but to do it. Drop the heavy bags of gossip, pretense, and resentments. Life improves and becomes lighter when we are sincere with our mate. I'm sitting way taller on my bed now, writing this tonight, thinking of when I was struggling with that box. It's not worth it, and even if my name was Jack, I wouldn't be in agreement with that statistic. Take my name off that list of the common lot.

It's too much to live for, even from where I sit. I can see the light now. I'm not settling for less no more. This thing, the way I see it, is a continuum—not a lay down and die. That's what being engulfed in hate boxes does. It makes you feel dead rather than alive with wellness and opulence as close family members. That backroom banter doesn't validate Obataiye. God Does! And He gave me the green light to lift off. He sent me the download when Dapper Dan gave me the breakdown on perseverance.

Lessons like that, in addition to those that followed all the way up to now, culminated in this book and those going to follow. I admit it was a close call to be so engulfed as I was in the hate box. I began to think in the negative daily and nightly while just lying in bed.

Thoughts of a vengeful mindset started to plague me. I knew that if I didn't plug into the power source of the Most High, self-destruction awaited me. That's exactly what did, and that was when those thoughts descended into oblivion.

We're not forced there.

When choices in the positive aren't affirmed than the negative, everything begins its myriad of destructive cycles. Drug abuse, dangerous lifestyle, and the list goes on and on. The devil never sleeps. He's working off the clock, and sometimes, through folks, we put on our clock by giving them the time of the day.

These days, I activate my vision by moving according to principles of optimum value. I go to school for one thing. It's an opportunity I have to get what I left at Schenley High School. I also go to the school of life within and without. There, I engage in studies that are revelatory and informative. I know now that a whole of well-wishing is contrived, fake, and dubious at best. I also predicate my moves on solidified knowledge, not guesswork or mere desire to fit into these boxes being thrown around. See, I shine the spotlight on my own actions and motives. I guess my process is synonymous with a highly effective refinery.

If you haven't noticed, my logic extends beyond the biological back to those who extend substance and sustenance to me. You guessed it, all of you. Yup, the Most High.

I'd be remiss not to give praise. You must be kidding me if you think I'd forget about my Maker and Sustainer through it all. Yes, those were mountains of boxes, but I know you've heard of faith the size of a mustard seed.

Those boxes are floating in the sea because they couldn't contain me, and I am not them, and Jack is not him. Even if I were Jack, I wouldn't have lacked. I serve the God of infinite life, opulence, light, and love. Love doesn't mean soft, mushy, or pushover; it's actually the opposite of being fretful. It takes courage to live in peace and pray for your enemies. It's a wasted life to project hate all day, every day, into your sleep, even your naps. That hate box is a serious predicament to be in.

Nothing but the dark one capitalizing off those caught up in Hateville, USA. Hearing the Holy Spirit guiding us tight with blaring static is practically impossible. The enemy wants us deaf like that.

Why?

Because faith comes by hearing the word. Faith is needed to cast off those mountains of boxes, remember?

Depression, paranoia, low self-esteem, gossip-mongering, and that wretched hate is the knife. The dark ones use the knife to cut off the inner ear of those bombarded and weighed down by boxes. Lo and behold, I finally lifted my sword—that word—that Holy Bible and fought to hear and to lift off. I heard that still small voice saying, "Now, go make footstools out of your obstacles." These days, I'm not asking folks not to judge me. I'm declaring that no one can judge me, especially when they're not judging themselves to see the impurities that need to be burned out of themselves. I tell the nay say and picture takers to take a snap of this.

Out with the old, in with the new, and no box can ever nor will ever hold me. My name is still Obataiye, not what they say. To those I'm kin to by spirit, I implore you to decide where you derive your self-worth from—your validation?

If your answer is not the creator, then you ain't saying Nathan. But that's another book. Pon intended—smile—no offense, brother Nathan. Vibe with me, though. You've been winning for a long time, and your victories are offensive to underachievers. I mentally recite Big Sis' slogan—Ms. Michelle Obama said when they go low, we go high. So let's fly all of you Nathans out there. Ain't no stopping us now. This is what we do. If you lose, they hate you for that, and they wonder why they're lost. That's deep.

January 17, 2023, I had shoulder replacement surgery, and it was the start of a new leg of my journey. Pun intended. Smile—take this rifle with me, right?

I left my cell and started off the unit before the surgery to go to the infirmary. As I left, my couple bros saluted as I reciprocate the love. We all agreed loudly that I was on my way to get a bionic shoulder. "See you when you get back, bro," they yelled out the steel bars, and my reply was, "Stay up y'all—I love y'all, bro."

On my way, I went with a C.O. escort down to the infirmary. I was sent off with assurance in my soul that this well-wishing and encouragement was official. Not only is this significant because it's the opposite of the note we're discussing, but these bros are from Philly.

This hateful jail culture over the years since way back has bred hate between Pittsburgh guys and Philly guys. In some prisons, during Steelers and Eagles games to thwart any royal rumbles, as they're called, when masses of dudes light out to fighting and rioting. This list goes on regarding the riff between our respective cities and cliques. However, the hate box has not always been successful at boxing up authentic camaraderie.

Even though there have been many boxing matches over the years involving our cities, we were living examples of camaraderie despite the expectation of us to fit in the geographical hate box. Although we have a force field around us that the hate can't penetrate, it's not a box.

To be sent off to a major surgery with solid, authentic support was and is major in itself. The injury to my shoulder happened in the late nineties at S.C.1., Cresson, while lifting weights. Over the years, it just got worse as I kept working out through the pain. I developed compound injuries to my shoulder as a result of going hard on myself. Best believe I paid in pain, too.

The MRI showed there was no cartilage in my shoulder. To think that I lifted weights practically right up to operation time. Admittedly, there was definitely some recklessness involved in my driving.

The stinginess y'all heard about relative to medical care, surgeries, etc., is true. However, I serve a God—the God that said: "Because he has set his love upon me, therefore, I will deliver him. I will set him on high because he has known my name; he shall call upon me, and I shall answer him."

The rest is obvious as you and I talk now, and you witness the Most High has satisfied me and showed me His salvation as He promised in Psalms 91—I'd never had surgery before this—let alone a replaced body part that was with me since birth. The night before the hospital trip was nerve-wracking as I cogitated being put in anesthesia. The thought even crossed my mind:

What if you don't wake up Obal…?

I thought it might not be such a bad thing—all this pain I've been feeling—honestly, I'm tired. Then my mom, grandma, little brother Jibreal, and the Holy Spirit said, "Quit those crazy thoughts but don't quit life. We don't do that."

I laid there looking for and beyond—batted my face with a serious look and nodded my head—while audibly saying, "Morning..." that's deep. I saw my little brother, mother, and grandmother's loving expressions, rooting for me to get on up. I agreed in my spirit and deepest recesses of my being, and this new leg of my journey began.

When I arrived at the hospital, the contemplation definitely intensified, but with a peace of mind that passed understanding. To me, the surgery prep and all that it entailed was further proof of my higher power being at the helm. The treatment was A1 everything. It was so official and outstanding that right before the surgery, as I was fading out of consciousness, the surgeon touched a part of my shoulder that obviously wasn't part of the deal. He said, "Does this hurt right here?" It wasn't hurting at the time, but it dawned on me that the part he touched pained me early in the mornings and throughout many sleepless nights, especially after working out. So I said, "Yeah, it does hurt." He demonstrated the size of the part, which was maybe an inch and a half; he said confidently and encouragingly, "I will take that out for you, and it will never bother you again."

I felt so blessed, yet I still drifted off. When I came to, I was discombobulated, to say the least. At the same time, deep inside, I could tell a part of me was restored. I also thought, *Yes, I can finally lift weights again without writhing in pain with every repetition.* Somehow, right there at the forefront of my thought world, even dizzy and dazed, I knew there was a deeper meaning to this journey.

From somewhere I couldn't see, the question was put forth to me.

Oba, will this be an interval of rest, or are you ready?

I answered in the affirmative.

I'm ready.

I insightfully gained some clarity relative to it all. When I say all—I mean the hate box, the dirt box, and every other box I'd dealt with and those they tried to throw me in.

Introspection was my chosen recourse as I left for the Great Pyramid at Giza for starters. My physical booty lay in Rockview's infirmary, but in the parallel, I descended to be revitalized. In the depths, I soon realized that these depths were different. There was a treasure in these depths that was intangible yet invaluable. This treasure trove consisted of the wisdom and understanding of descending to ascend. I mined a brand new valuation of myself. I was reminded down there that I am too valuable to kill myself by entertaining the falsities of the false. I was, for many years, losing life slowly by my harmful actions and non-actions, for that matter. To be stagnant is to die in place with everybody else's boxes over the top of you.

The brightest light I'd ever seen shone through the narrow shaft, containing a message.

Set on up, Taiye, activate your vision again. Remember Dapper Dan?

Perseverance lives in you my son.

Habitual sins and vices, hate, muck, and mire are all designed to block God's blessings. At this time, we render those principalities defeated and nailed to the cross. Everybody has their minuscule ideas of who they think you are and what box you fit in. We declare those ideas to be false and very insignificant.

Down in the great, it dawned on me that I needed to let go of the old ways of thinking and concentrating on nonsense. Those fiery darts sting, but inside, I found and tapped into the power to quench those fiery darts. I decided it was time to move on to the next level of my trip.

I lay there in silence until their meals came through. Not having my tangibles, such as commissary, cosmetics, etc., was slightly adverse, but it added to the urgency to finally get my mind right. Where else could I be but recharging in the vast Greatness of a structure that pointed me to God? The 80" flat screen was gigantic in my house. It had its part to play, too—besides movies. I'm not a movie buff these days for obvious reasons. It was time to learn and master Activision. True to form, I watched this ESPN piece. Featured was a young athlete named Brandon Graham, who shared how he inspires kids in America who fall on hard times to feel good about themselves in spite of their circumstances. Most of them were handicapped physically and emotionally until he emerged in their lives, exuding love for them. Do I have to tell you that I dropped a few seats instantly as I vibed with the moving parts of that documentary? Moving parts are love in action, which is undoubtedly hands down but not handicapped—the direct opposite of hate.

That's the light shining through to me again; I thought as I deeply pondered about what I had just witnessed. Being surrounded by so much bad energy for so long, seemingly at every turn of the way, makes one doubt love exists sometimes.

But stories and examples like that are the value of stick-to-it-ive-ness is inestimable. I went into the bathroom, looked in the mirror, and said, "Yeah, nowhere near over."

Not only is there the light of love in, but it's still around. It was just my view was obscured because I let my guard down. Most importantly, I was being reminded that my connection to the Most High was alive and valid. The reputation I once had took major hits for sure. In fact, it was obliterated; however, so was my shoulder.

Early in my life, I'd been under attack from the evilest to do it. He sent touchers at me under the guise of love, although mate was at the core of it all. I'm sure I was affected in a myriad of harmful ways. Next, that sucka sent drug abuse disguised as good times and promises. He sent plagues, divorce, dissension, pornography, gambling, strife, malice, guns, and even swiped my mom, baby bro, and grandmother, all while I was already submerged in grief.

Aaaah... but there is a God that I am the temple of, and one thing is certain: there is the Father, and surely there is the Word, and He's the resurrection. So that old reputation was nailed to the cross with all the other muck and mire. Even the old shoulder is gone to hurt no more. This is a new day y'all. This is Obataiye aaaaaaaaaaaaand still.

That inner me hasn't been damaged in the least bit; in fact, it's been enriched with even more compassion than before. More respect for my fellow human beings, more willingness to lend a helping hand to the unknown, not just a known associate or a popular person. See, it's all about the new now. That old then got me here. Well, I've stalked through the valley of the shadow of death and fear. Look into the tomb they made for me. After I got up and out, I pushed on through the foliage and rough weather straight to the highest peak in P.A. Once there, I looked way out to lift off central. That still small voice in me said if you can see there, you can be there. I agreed and continued my ascent.

Even in a progressive motion, I must admit that every now and then, I glance through to remind myself that lessons in those losses were the prerequisite for these wins. Even if my name was Jack—I will not be contained.

No more boxes!

What do I look like except who the Most High made me to be, huh? I'm not fitting into this horrible box in spite of the millions that flock to it. Even after observing and experiencing the tragic effects of division and hate, follies still run to it.

All the shootings are symptoms of hate, just like arthritis, heart attacks, and diseases are. Yup, research it. It's very insidious. Self-hate, or I hate how he walks, or she looks… are all secret thoughts of a hater. Who does he thinks he is? It's all hate.

THE COMMON STAT BOX

EVERYTHING FROM ADDICT TO PUSHER

I'm thinking never to say die unless it's to them old ways, brethren. While, we're at it, them old ways of thinking too. There are specific lower-level attacks from those dark regional forces. Those forces definitely work through people, too. Of course, the weapons are boxes, and I've been picking apart the common statistic box.

We must make ourselves impervious to these attacks. While they were plotting on me, I was plotting on them and learning those ways and means. The ways are duplicated over and over again, but they are only different in form. The means are largely vices and low-impulse habits designed to block our blessings. I've been immersed in so much pain due to disappointing myself that my awareness is imperative. This common stat box is definitely a bully box. Its immenseness is mostly hidden despite its size. Ironically, it's so common that it's practically invisible.

I got a download, and it's a high-level native version. Pure love, merged with intelligence, are the bully slayer. So, nowadays, we acquire the right knowledge, use it to grow, and go, never to return to the regurgitation that is the common lot.

Year after year, stretching way back to the 80s, according to my memory, it's been almost regular for black mates to get caught right in the gunplay box, yet consequences are so high. There is no plaything in the stat: Guns kill more people than cars. That might not seem so astounding until we break down the fact that guns outnumber cars 3 to 1. Cars are flying around everywhere in every locality, outskirts, small towns, and some more, yet guns still slaughter far more people. Now, I'm not one of these people who think guns should be banned; however, recklessness should be banned. In all wariness, I was reckless, to say the least, although I've dealt with mental issues from childhood. I still accept responsibility for my wrongful actions. I undeniably contributed to this ugly stat box. Dare I say I fret the very thought of this stat box?

They're getting lowered six feet underground way too early, way too much, and often. I don't fear death - it's being caught up in the atmospheric pressure and pain it causes. That's just the reason why when I waltzed through the valley of fear and death, I stopped, meditated, took seven deep breaths, then I left.

The numbers are astronomical of people who miss out on invaluable opportunities, messing around in these boxes and ending up statistics one way or the other. These are folks whose profession it is to determine within what radius people die relative to the hood. The nerve is empowering to me these days.

My whole thing is how dare they feel like they can predict my moves and get it right.

The only thing I beg is to differ.

We deprive ourselves of feeding our souls right when we fail to do the right thing, just like they say and write - like they're right. Good soul food for me these days is the right knowledge, and I constantly use it. I don't do drugs anymore. That's too common and statistical- I crave good living, laughing, and loving - can I add learning? Right, learning. Let's lift off, y'all. They can't put any box on something that's tight, you heard? We should never restrict ourselves by these statistics! Lines that are so blurred. I say blurred to mean corny. That's what that knowledge does. We begin to see clearly when we work on it and view it through its lenses. What used to have us lost due to the lenses' opaqueness is now transparent.

Even when they throw an ambiguous box at us, they only succeed in confusing themselves. It's like a weak game in the jailhouse, where flattery is the feature film to the knowledgeable. At the end of the longest soliloquy, a soup is sought. I give the soup up, smiling, and throw some corn in that dip. No pun intended. Yes, it is - smile with me, y'all. Let's keep going, though.

It's good every now and then to have a mental movie playback. I've starred in sequels of Crazies film productions. It literally takes me to play back the consequences of starring in those films. The supporting cast didn't stick around when the smoke cleared, and every time, I felt like a bully in the end. Come on, y'all - you know what I'm talking about. Common lot box games have serious potential to go all the way left. So, to push play is to dig deep and connect with the peace that surpasses understanding. A lot of the time, though, I just pray.

My primary frame of reference these days is those old films. From where I sit, you can say I'm the owner of the old production company, and I'm paying our very costly dividends. All the investors are eating, too; mightily, if I may add.

Some of the investors are barely grown, yet they have an authority over me that I gave them. It's to the point where most of them don't even feel right telling me to go ahead and lock up. They're just as shocked and embarrassed as me half the time because, as common as it's become, it's odd. Kings, bosses, stars, master poets, architects, rocket scientists, even. Yes, even them. Geniuses, engineers, true pioneers of greatness locked in cages - commonly referred to as just another number. To their credit, though, I do remember some teachers in grade school warning us kids not to become the common statistic that is the jailbird that sings oldies out the cell door better than the original singer. This is common, folks. I've lived it and am still living it through my perspective, which has changed.

This change occurred deep in my thought life, as that's where everything is formulated. There's no way in the world I could've lived through, observed, and analyzed all that I did, and do, and still go on as a common one or better, yet a statistic that's cool with being just that. To be lost in this system is common, as sad as this may be. It's a common reality and box that just sits there sometimes. We've all been guilty of just jumping into this box of grief. I'm recalibrating these days. I'm yelling out, "Ignite the lights." The atmospheric pressure exists on heavy levels, but to fold is to die. Instead, I convert the pressure to fuel and link up with the rocket scientist and like-minded. We're operating at high levels too. It's only right to go high, though. When it becomes common to catch folks looking at you with jealousy and envy out of a side eye, that's my cue to exit upward-bound.

Some of these guys are durable enough to frequently say, "I love you, bro." Very common, too. This I-love-you thing is like a phenomenon these days. A lot of times, the ones saying it are the most jealous and hateful, and they seem to think they're undetectable. Oh, so common!

It's all empowering and very impactful. To constantly run into box-throwers is one thing, but when others do as if they like you, they try to incarcerate you with another box. What, the small box of cell wasn't enough of a box? Seeing and feeling the potency of such dishonesty for me was a game-changer. I guess you can say that I became an emergency construction worker. That's that company owner in me again, coming to the forefront. "Taiye's Construction." I'm not only the owner but also putting the work in. I'm specializing in building myself back up even better than before.

Here at Taiye's Constriction, I'm also building bridges from prison to passion, which is freedom. This time, I'm paying my dividends to the Most High because He's worthy. Partnering with my Lord and Savior, Jesus Christ, ensures that I never deconstruct or negatively influence myself. From January to April, I was in the presence of guys with ailments as serious as terminal cancer. I made sure not to take that time for granted. Yet again, I was directed by that still small voice to be still and pay attention. Close attention, too. Not just a glance but a peering into the circumstances I was facing.

To continue to complain about anything would be victimization after witnessing folks who themselves expected to die soon. How ungrateful it would be if I didn't vibe with those guys? I sat and talked with most of them from time to time. I prayed with them and for them in private time. I couldn't help but feel for those guys, and I often thought about how they were caught up in this statistical box. I repeatedly implored them to believe their way out of that box and to pray earnestly like never before.

The point I'd seen in their eyes I also heard in their voices. Was it so different if I didn't muster everything I had in me to rebuild and get on top of my circumstances? The relatability existed between us so powerfully because, in fact, I lived like I was dying inside like they did. Often, I feel like getting even. Violent thoughts plagued me, trying to get me to just thug it out. Redeem your name – redeem your name - you're losing it, Obataiye. Everybody thinks you're a fraud - a punk, a coward, some type of trench. That's when, once again, I knew I had to dig deeper into myself. When those negative thoughts get to buzzing like bees and flies, the need is bigger than insecticide. It's all about the power of 'choice' these days. To keep choosing wrong is synonymous with slow or possibly suicide.

Dreams die almost instantaneously in guys with bad decisions. Decisions made in anger, shame, pride, and haste. All for what? to prove a point, right? How very common is that box? Most of the time, these occurrences in this common statistical box are a direct result of our not knowing how to endure pain and make it work out for us. Growth is trying to burst through if we just make the right choice and mast the gas. "No pain, no gain." Sometimes, we gain and don't know it until we deflect. Muscles endure pain and adversity while what? Growing out of the box! Upon my analysis, I've realized that we are plunged into a big pool of unnecessary competition. This pool engulfs many times over the Olympic pools, and would-be Olympians too. Nay, before it even gets to the guns and violence, there's a poisonous effect on everyone involved. I'm tired of it all, but the good kind of tired. Not the guilty kind. Winners never quit, and quitters never win.

And I've realized there's no need to compete because I'm already a success. To compete or even conceive it mentally is akin to competing against myself. It seems like most people are competing with even their closest friends and relatives. This is frenemy action in truth or, rather, lies. Always in competition mode goes hand in hand with envy and jealousy.

It's so bad and petty that positive change in a person provokes some to hate you. I faced, and presently face a lot of opposition merely for changing and transcending to an elevated mind state. Who in their right mind would want to scrape along the same old sidewalks in caterpillar fashion when we could form wings and take flight by choice? Sometimes, the blowback of the hidden resentments was so potent that the negative energy affected me horribly. When it catches you off guard because of who the hate and jealousy come from, it can be dizzying.

Trying to make sense of it all and wondering how folks would oppose even slightly - a positive change in a neighbor or a friend. Even family will look at you like you're crazy. In times like that, I encountered writer's block as I descended into dark clouds. I became mean, defensive, and vengeful. Then I caught myself, supplicated and prayed fervently, as implored by the mighty like-minded prayer warriors of the Most High. My whole thing now is unequivocal: I will no longer fit in anyone's common stat box. It's been too many lessons unfolding to me, specifically for me, to keep a faulty trajectory going. Depression, serious drug use, jail, alcoholism, and shooting everything up, including my own, has to be a turning point. Now, granted, it's hard to stop once you are engaged full throttle in any of the aforementioned. One thing I know well is that our Father in the heavens and in us gives each of us many moments of clarity. That's our "Cue" to get out of the box and into the positive energy flow that tugs at us in private. That still small voice that whispers and, at other times, yells at us to do better. Just thinking about all those pitfalls and boxes makes me shake my head and say to myself and to the world - there's no way in this world I'd stay stuck or jump back in anyone's box.

Musingly, I recalibrate as I long these days to use my God-given capabilities that I'm in my right mind.

There's no stopping now as I catch a new kind of steam. Well, it's not new, but in my case, it's just been unused until now. So, I actually tip my hat to all my haters and naysayers who sent their vibes my way. Those vibes were static, but I converted them into dynamic energy. One thing they won't call me is Jack-in-the-Box.

Statistics say that hate, jealousy, envy, resentment, and stress will surely manifest in the bodies of those who entertain them. All that madness destroys smiles, dreams, and, a lot of times, lives. I lived it, and the boxes still come flying into this day. I will be bobbing and weaving and then taking flight when I supplicate and give God the glory. I couldn't mention The Most High too many times because He lifted me up way more than I could mention and praise Him. My maker - your maker - He made boxes, just not the ones we've been struggling with on our journey. He only gives us opportunities, and they come unceasingly.

Now, He gave each of us our toolbox, and it's full if we only know it.

Some do know, but again, to know and not do only amounts to - well, nothing, or perhaps the jailhouse. God forbid the death box because He came to give us eternal life. He fought death and won, remember. Now, we've got to use these tools before they melt into the box from atrophy. The calamitous nature of all those boxes flying in at us is certainly traumatic. However, we must take heed to our higher selves and springboard off the springs in the calamity. From experience, I know there's always an opportunity on the other side of the storm. The fresh levels of soil that ensue are super fertile for the seeds in idea form that we gather in adversity. I do get that sometimes we have to wait our turn. At the same time, putting too much weight on the wait means stagnating. Stagnation is akin to death, movement is to be alive while we strive. Now, positive movement is to be alive, plus some. Personally, I had to refocus and figure out how to aim at my goals in life.

I had to keep my mind in its proper gear to be sure it didn't slip into reverse. Gears grind to a halt when that happens. And, yeah, so like Dapper the O.G. told me when I was 12, "Perseverance is key." Learn the word, realize its essence, and fly like a bird. No box can hold me, and it's now even logical, but it's built into my biological to overcome all obstacles. At this juncture, it's my understanding that perseverance contributes greatly to self-mastery. We have to master ourselves before we can master our trades, crafts, and talents.

King Solomon said the way up is down, but we're not to stay down. Boxes and obstacles, such as alibis, are not cutting for Obataiye. To always live in Excuseville, Pa., obliterates perseverance and determination. You'll look up one day and find the box enclosed on all sides, where there used to be a flap to bust out of. Now that thing's sealed. "Not I." Common statistic who? I'm off that, sistren and brethren, youngins and ole heads. We've got to make a change for the better. Upon harnessing our will via self-mastery, we'll definitely deprive the grave instead of feeding it with our beloved people and children. Statistics that hurt to the point of no return. Now, there are mass shootings in massive numbers daily in our beautiful America. Come on now. We've got to do better than this. We have what many people abroad would die for, for lack of a better term, yet the term used is befitting. Many people die on their trek here to America the Great. Although the courage within is tapped into and utilized to scale and overcome these walls of the stat box, we can overcome all these boxes.

Those of us who aren't desensitized have to link up even if the conduit is the ether by itself. Positivity attracts other positive ideas and folks who are moving in similar lanes, countries, and even worldwide, especially with the internet in full operation. Once we start to subordinate the fake and false ornate, we transcend to higher frequencies and synergize. There is a potent opaqueness within the box life.

This absence of light is favorable to box proliferation of the worst kind. It will continue on a negative course; life will until we say enough is enough.

It starts with us right now as soon as you scratch your head like that's a good point. That's one of the moments of clarity we spoke about earlier. It was taught if you can see it, you can be it. Now, be careful to see right because it works for the worst as well as the better visions.

Reading, writing, and comprehending what's going on with us are powerful opportunities, too, but premium opportunities, once realized, require premium output.

We should be incredibly motivated these days with all the potential we possess. To know, though, we've got to grow. The muck and the mire, from the box with the sand to the present man. From the black and white and black barbie dolls, you've grown into a woman who's better than any barbie. We figure it out as we go as long as we grow, though. Can't stay stuck.

Buckle in, now lift off. It's either skyward bound or an implosion in the statistics box. That's a violent collapse inward that can surely be averted right now because it is first who we were made to be. That's to connect with the Most High and just see what's next. Blessed up!

At the end of the day, after knowing better, to implode would be self-imposed. Now, real talk, the ills we've suffered are legitimate reasons and causes for our plight to a certain extent.

There is no excuse for staying stuck.

Its knobby tires are available to us, especially since the Almighty stoops low for those who were stuck and thought to be last. He'll wake us first to the utter surprise of all naysayers. The adequacy is in us to begin as we just have to trust the process as opposed to losing all trust; thus, hope is lost. It's about where I place my trust now and in who, and sorely, is not in anybody's box.

Even if my name was Jack, y'all. I stand too tall to be squished in these boxes they put my name on. They've wasted time that could've been spent getting their minds right when I started getting mine right.

If you're reading this, I guarantee you've got great ability, just like the top achievers in your scope. That's why that voice in you is nudging you to step your game up, athlete. This arena called life is real, and so are the prizes involved. With great ability in action, we make possibilities more probable, ever recognizing that with God, we are unstoppable.

This is the logic that our haters lack; it's simply the facts: Big Facts! I took the letters from the word "excuse," mixed with the ability, and added them to my springboard. Then I meditated, and my inner man said, "Buckle in and lift off."

It's too common to keep falling off by the wayside, addicted to this, that, and the other. We should teach our kids, especially our daughters, how to prepare for welfare. We teach our sons to prepare for a peddling life, and I'm not talking about mountain bikes. The mountains, yeah, but the ones with the prisons. It's of great importance that we break away from the pressure to be just like everybody else in our scope—putting investments of our precious thought life into worrying about what others are doing and how they view our uniqueness.

Lost in the sauce, one can literally start to hate their uniqueness. Come to find out the sauce, one can start to hate their uniqueness. I came to find out that the sauce is not only generic but nasty, too. Some generic items were good back in the day, I do admit. The big black and white labels were jumping off the shelf. Those days are long gone, though, and it's time for that inner beauty to do its duty, brethren. Enough is enough. The babies are dying in swaths. They are putting fentanyl in weed pills that look like candy. What's next?

Our best qualities are immobilized by the need to fit into the stat box. In turn, our worst is released after heating up and metastasizing from the pressurized effect of being squished in that little old box with our big ole wings tightly tucked into our sides. They weren't meant to be tucked. They might as well be plucked thin if we're just going to squeeze them into box after box after box. It makes sense to keep frustrating ourselves chasing illusions and false victories, only to end up dead or in prison or still out on the streets or in your house in prison.

That type of frustration leads to self-loathing, which can beget negative outbursts, addictions, depression, and mental illness. At that point, the best plans go up in smoke. Hopefully, not gun smoke, meth smoke, crack smoke, or chimney smoke up in these mountains. The illusionary car comes to a screeching halt, and whiplash ensues.

I peered in and figured out that my combinativeness wasn't necessarily bad.

Its flipside is now recognized as an indomitable will. Like the one you've got. You're mean because your inner self is trying to do what it's meant to do: take flight. But you keep trapping them in the box.

Mad for nothing? Evil person, no. Loser?

Not at all.

Complete idiot or reprobate? Not by a long shot.

It's just the real you trying to be free, but the box confuses and angers them, just like the jailbirds in the mountains and hills. Brethren, conceive this and believe this. We are endowed with and blessed with success already. It's just a matter of tapping into our best selves instead of tapping out. It can be no mystery why the youth go the way they go. It starts with us. The supposed-to-be fathers and sometimes mothers. We all collectively have to assume the responsibility.

If we don't control ourselves and our minds, we permit ourselves to be controlled by the box. The box begets all types of adverse effects, from drug addiction to immoral sex, guns, self-hate, and disunity, in a nutshell, no pun intended.

I recently observed an encouraging unfolding on the subject of self-control and being firm in the right character. It was in class here at Rockview. There were two younger guys off a different block than mine. They're on the same block, and one, out of nowhere, started basically berating and harassing the other guy, saying, "Why couldn't you sync my tablet up to the kiosk last night, dawg?" The other guy replied, "Because the C.O.s were observing the kiosk, and they were off-limits at the time you wanted to be synced up." So the other guy wouldn't accept that answer, and he just kept coming from slightly different angles but asking the same question with a pressuring tone. But the guy who refused to sync the guy's tablet kept stating his position assertively that he wasn't about to get into a dispute with the C.O.s about a tablet that wasn't his. But the "pressure dude" wouldn't take the explanation. The guy who refused to sync up the tablet wasn't from PA, I have to mention.

A lot of times, "out-of-towners" will feel pressured and timid; this guy held his ground, telling Mr. Pressure, "Listen, man, I was supposed to put myself in harm's way for you?" he reasoned assertively. And "Pressure Guy" persisted, "Man, you could've synced my tablet up." But the "out-of-towner" kept his cool and confident composure and repeatedly stated his position until the teacher halted the discussion. I had been paused in my work in silent admiration of this young out-of-towner and fellow levitator's indomitable will. He refused to compromise, even against the odds and far away from his home state.

Obviously, this guy was in prison for whatever reason; however, he had a moral code that someone instilled in him, even though he forfeited his freedom. We don't have to be defined by our mistakes and bad choices. There is hope, even when there are many bad choices, but only if we can see that far. So many times, as younger people, we've fallen victim to myopic syndrome. Only being able to see what's directly in front of us. Our bigger picture-seeing ability is impeded when those immediate circumstances and adversities unfold. A lecture here and there is futile in any attempt at straightening the course of the runaway mental vessel.

This is where we come in. Those of us who see, feel, and comprehend the wrongs. In fact, we've perpetuated many of them while the babies that are now running amok watched. I'm compelled to do more than just complain about how today's youngins are so crazy, or the world is so off the chain, etc. Love conquers hate, and at the core of this life thing, it's about loving ourselves enough to love others, especially God, and in this love is the change. Love is the alchemist, if you will. It fortifies my mind from the box-throwers and the boxes themselves.

Those of us who are older now can and must find it in us to recommit ourselves. To be purposeless is to be lifeless. It's that deep. To be purposeless is to jump on the "blue goose" for free, except for the bus fare of your freedom. I paid my bus fare a couple of times, and they were glad to accept my payment. The steaks, the bacon, the car and house notes, their kids' schooling - it's on me. I forgot to mention that the big RV I often dream of owning is riding cross-country in multiples annually. And for what? All for the sake of the statistic box and all those other boxes I was in and out of. Well, I'm tired of it, so I'm breaking the trend. I welcome you and challenge you to challenge your lower impulses and levitate over the boxes as they come. They come in fast and slow every day from every angle and direction. The fast ones seem to have a mind of their own and think we didn't notice them. The slow ones try to trick us into believing they don't exist and sometimes are invisible. Until we're caught up inside and the form appears out of nowhere. The nights are cold and lonely after a while. At first, it might be some fun here and there, but it's short-lived.

Just ask all the homeless folks across the country. The drug addicts, and yup, you guessed it, the jailbirds that took the goose when it set the GPS for the mountains. On a higher note than the goose could fly, though, there are no limits except those we acknowledge. Those boxes, people's labels, and expectations, those prison cells can only limit or stop those with myopia. Those who can't see past the difficulties will inevitably see themselves in the stat box. Let's be their eyes and shoulders as we extend our vision.

THE HEDONIST BOX

Now, whether we're careful or not, this area of life is tricky. The boxes are multitudinous in this context alone. As children, the draw starts with those Similac shakes that look vanilla, but nope - and it doesn't matter. They're going down the hatch steadily. We tried to slurp them down without even breathing at times. Now, that's some serious pleasure there, along with the hunger. And had no problems bursting out in tears if it took too long to resume shake inhalation onslaught.

As we grew, so did the variety of morsels we devoured. Some of us were allowed to delve into the candy realm, but it inevitably spiraled into more than just a delve. More like sticky faces, hands, clothes, and everything we touched or trekked. Through every part of the house, even the bathroom toilet was fair game. Big ole bowl of water. Might as well get this melted cherry blow pop off my hands. Dad, mom, and gram would come through and frantically grab you before you drown. I guess the big-eyed look while smacking at the bowl looked a little dangerous. "Get him before he jumps in there," I guess would be the thought, especially if Ma Dukes was off on that "J." Pleasure was, and is a need and want for every human being alive. This includes parents, as many of us know, first and second-hand. In fact, many of us have gleaned some of our indulgences from our parents. This was funny and cute until, slowly but surely, Lil Boopy metastasized into a full-blown addict.

Sad but true, Ma smoked pleasure, taught the baby in like, and everybody laughed out loud until the guns came out. Yes, it gets that deep, brethren and sistren. All for the sake of pleasure can be a life preserver. Laughter is a top-shelf medicine for sure when it's healthy. When it comes in box form, watch out for the incoming. You might get your head boxed off.

Speaking for myself, I was a baby weed head. In fact, the aforementioned baby; however, my mom was a baby too. I defend my mom; may she rest in peace. She didn't understand life like she started to before she passed. I was her first child, and she was in her early 20s when I was born. My dad and her were married but divorced almost just as fast. Ma Dukes was very beautiful and told just that all the time, too. All those compliments and the atmosphere of the hood formulated the perfect storm. Young folks need to be valued primarily for who they are on the inside. Early reinforcement of character, integrity, intelligence, and love is highly imperative. Ahh, she was so cute, or he was so cute. Of course, he is very kind, especially when it's very obvious. However, we as adult caregivers and parents must be aware of the need to instill that proper humility in our youth. To be down to earth, if you will, keeps the head from inflating. When this inflating of the head or the ego occurs, that's when we float right into a big ole box, bigger than our ego and head.

The kids fit, too, and whoever else follows out of sheer need or admiration. We never hurt only ourselves. Look back in the wake of the vessel that is ourselves and the box we rode in on. If you're honest, you'll see and say exactly what we all see with our own eyes. All this madness has been inherited, infused, circulated, and perpetuated in some way, shape, form, or fashion. If you're honest, you'd admit we've all contributed somehow, even if our contribution was minimal or unknowing, it's there now. The beauty of it all is that we have, as individuals, a power instilled in us by the Most High. By ourselves, we accomplished private victories, small as they may be, the largeness is in the unseen, intangible things. When you put the cigarettes down - big win - you haven't drunk alcohol for seven years after fooling and bar-hopping for decades - big win - and you - You stopped smoking crack and sniffing heroin, not to mention you're holding onto your job. Big Things for Big Folks. Now do this: envision what we can do collectively as it relates to correcting the incorrect problems on this big test called America.

It starts with us because we are here now and cognizant of what our needs are. Box-free love, kindness, good sense, principled thinking, and activism. Out with the selfishness and the poisonous egotism. All those guys are egos, pain, baby addicts, disappointment, hopelessness, and misdirection. 'We've been duped into believing in nonstop partying, fun, kee-keeing, and chemicalizing our minds, bodies, and souls to the point of literal sickness. There's more to it - this life thing is precious and strong, but fragile. The line is thin, and when we are not careful, everything is lost when the mind blows, even when it lives sometimes. This is unacceptable as far as I'm concerned. The Most High did not create us to be housed in no boxes of mediocrity, addictions of all sorts, or lower impulse pleasures.

Hyenas are the only other species on the planet that kee-kees while being devoured. Those lions get to ripping, and the Hyenas just giggle out of consciousness. It's really analogous to us sometimes. Everything is a joke and a party, even in the face of destruction. "Self-destruction, even."

According to I Peter 5:8, "Be sober, be vigilant; because your adversary the devil walks around like a roaring lion seeking whom he may devour." So we see here that 2,000 years ago, and probably further back, temptations were in more than just the islands. The pleasure box spreads far and wide, reaching into our homes and minds. It's almost baffling if it wasn't so obvious at times. The pleasure box doesn't always disguise itself, or the thrower of the box doesn't always dumb it down. This thing relies on us being The Jack in the Box type who can't resist. It banks its hopes on us being easily led to the slaughter due to hopelessness.

How long will we stay the course? Even in the game of golf, it's a given that, at times, the golf ball will be inadvertently driven off course. However, the course is still the objective for ultimate success, which can be obtained by correctly navigating. The difference between us often is that we'll slip off course, which happens in life, but then we'll stay on the wrong course. Even knowing the chances usually entails pain, injury, loss, even jail, and sometimes death. Extreme, yes, but oh so true too many times. The talent and genius in this one jail are very extensive, not to mention the multitudinous jails and, in fact, graveyards too. From piano players to architects, teachers, electricians, photographers, motivational speakers, playwrights, directors, and master builders, the list goes on and on between here and the graveyard. Yes, that space between is our conscious effort to break the cycle.

There's so much more to life, and yes, hindsight is 20/20, but I felt a sense of doom when I was high growing up. I never spoke about it, but I often felt a literal sense of doom that words can't express. Those feelings were intuition and God warning me.

A lot, if not most times, the struggle out there is real, but our actions and inaction make it real and harder to overcome. Too much pleasure-seeking is a sure way to lose focus, especially for under-privileged folks. The disadvantages are obvious; however, hurdles get leaped over at the track and field. We are in that track and field, so I say let's get to leaping like the many victorious supposedly disadvantages. These disadvantages are like weightlifting.

Let's work out with the best of them and press on toward the prize. The prize could be peace in a home bought and paid for on some decent land. Your prize could be an apartment with all the amenities overlooking the city, an Audi A8 in the garage, and a beautiful wife. Your prize could be that studio you imagined owning when you were 13 years old in the cultural district of your city. Yours could be that brand new RV equipped to haul your motorcycles cross-country at will. Or yours could be to run restaurants and food trucks by the fleet, maybe a real estate guy or girl. Whatever your prize is in life, it will not be attained in the box of pleasure. Get out of those forsaken boxes, which are traps to discombobulate us. Enough is enough, brothers and sisters of every race.

The time is now. I'm tired of being sick and tired. Even with these couple of grays I have, resigning to a life of bedazzlement and being high and drunk all the time is not an option. I want to experience the mountains where the jails aren't. I know there are some better mountains than these penitentiary, riddled hills. All the flash-in-the-pan pleasures lead to a raw deal every time in some way.

To be cooking out on that lakefront property is your brightest idea manifested. Now that's pleasure, that's right, and well done. Black folks are not the only ones who like it well done, ya know. Those minute pleasures that cause so much turmoil in our lives have to go. I would call them insignificant if they didn't cause so much pain and eventual loss. The babies lose out big time when their protectors leave for the mountains without them. Leaving them fifty times a week is bad enough. About next to nothing, we keep leaving those little bundles of joy. They looked just like us as the tears streamed down their cheeks, which we had given them. Is there really any wonder why they rebelled and acted up? Frustrated, abandoned, and hurt without truly understanding why.

Maybe mommy will see just how much I miss her if I walk behind her. These creeps on the corner don't deserve or reserve the right to watch my mom's rear end. On top of that, I might as well frown at them to let them know I'm reppin' me and my dad.

Sistren and brethren, these are facts that have to be dealt with accordingly. There's not that much getting high and drunk in the world. Yes, it took me to lose it all and land in prison. But it doesn't have to cost you any more than hopefully the price of this book.

From where I sit, the rearview mirror is really hard to avoid most of the time. It's very true that we shouldn't steer too long into the past. However, to pick up the pieces of the broken mirrors and my life, I have to at least gaze back so I don't get cut anymore. I chased the pleasure box for so many years that it became second nature. Once, I landed in prison, even in my earlier jail stints, it was all about the cigarettes and other commissary. Scoring a walkman radio was usually a big deal, too. The radio only served to reminisce longingly about the hybridized pleasure/pain we left in the streets. Other than this twisted yearning to go and self-destruct, the walkman radio would be invisible in the free world.

But only to the over-hip folks. I never ran into all those who kept it simple in these jails, up state or county jails. Maybe a couple of "keep it simple guys" made very short county bids. Like a week or two, if that. I can't help but ponder the many folks who made all their family reunions and cookouts. Class reunions, kids' birthdays, their own birthdays and holidays. I admit, at this point, I am definitely a jailbird, but I'm no ordinary bird. I'm an Eagle. A Bald Eagle – lol - but an Eagle all the same. Thanks to the unction of The Holy Spirit of The Most High. I'm keying into this keen insight nowadays. I can see the runway clearly and the limitless sky. So now, it's all about cleaning and preparing my wings for takeoff. Call me Bald Eagle-eyed Obataiye, but you'll no longer call me Jack in the Box. Last week, on the news, they reported on four shark attacks within two days on the same beach.

I thought how analogous this scenario was to the pleasure subterfuge of the devil. Furthermore, how totally insane it was and is to ignore the example laid out plainly before us, yet, we run off the cliff into a college of sharks. It's not an ordinary school, but smart sharks that have honed in on our sleepwalking habits. Or shall we say "sleep swimming" with the fish? It's pretty easy picking when everyone is doing the same things, at the same times, day in and day out. The traps have been set, and some we set for ourselves, then write songs glorifying the tactics used to trap us while paradoxically in the trap. I feel so crazy and tricked sometimes. I think, "This had to be a fluke," and/or I'll wake up at home to gram's chicken cooking at 706 Webster Terrace in "86." But when I look at all these scars, those seen and unseen, and also all those damned bars and realize, nope, no more gram's chicken Taiye. Those times and chances have expired. Now, grandma smiles down on me and within my eyes and soul as she roots for me to go for mine now that I'm not blind. I see clearly how all that time I thought I was going somewhere, slickly. But the game and the devil were the station and the can of oil. I was building walls with all those bricks I threw at this place where I now sit. However, I move with relentless persistence out from the muck and mire of Boxville, U.S.A.

I'm no longer interested in even the glamorous stories of the battles and the tearing down of the bridges; I should've been fortifying and extending them. There is a certain power of perpetuation in storytelling in which we relive what enslaved us. I tend to stay away from such gatherings unless I'm shedding some light into those darkened places and shadowy ciphers.

Jesus has me so driven these days that it's imperative for me to subordinate the ride-or-die mentality. The beast mode mentality lurks in those darker places. The very places that make the earth gape open are full of early graves. I don't take, nor do I see the pleasure in generations being slaughtered by the wayside of life. And to think I get hated because of my new positive approach to life. It's true, as a lot of you have experienced. To be exceptional in an age of boxology or nothing is challenging. Some people even want to harm me in any way they can, but they know I have a history and possibly a button. The whole ordeal causes confusion because bullies want it easy, and I'm Psalms 91, equipped. Plus, I might just have a button too. They don't know?

Some take great pleasure in hating; however, for us to become as hateful as our haters, there would be no winners. And I like to win, and I know you do too; that's why you read more these days about winning, and slowly but surely, you're doing less losing. I'm not entertaining any hate on purpose. Although, they must get something out of watching us so intently. Keep on shining, brothers and sisters, because I am, regardless of the dark. I bring a spark, then an all-out light for the good fight. And I'm all in. Hold up now, I'm not in nobody's box, and my name is not Jack. It's Obataiye. When I say in it, I'm talking about life in abundance that only God can give. Buckle in with me, y'all. It's time to hone in on our gifts, the main present being the present now lifted off.

Hedonism is defined as the doctrine that pleasure is the chief good in life. When we overindulge in simple pleasures, danger looms as pleasure turns into vice. In the tightening of these vices is the muck of being stuck. That activism we once embodied so gracefully exits the building that is our very being. Then comes the darker shades and the illest thoughts, like, "life is played out." To think life is played out is not only very profound to ponder but also a sad state of mind. Sad but preventable, sistren and brethren. True story: these are the demonic thoughts in the ether just searching for the hopeless souls to connect with.

When I was but a small child, I used to shake my legs, not really conscious of it. You know how you can be just sitting and zoned out, or in and be shaking your legs really fast, or tapping your heel on the floor. Well, mom, may she rest in peace, used to tell me to "Stop doing that, Oba. It doesn't look right, and it's not good for you, baby." I truly believe my mom instinctively and intuitively knew that I was dissipating vital energy. Seemingly insignificant, this concept is when we are devoid of proper insight. We need all the energy we can muster to stay mentally, physically, and spiritually fortified. The struggles are real; the issues we face as human beings are substantial without all these boxes. Now add the weight, especially of the avoidable. It's a matter of great importance that we address.

Countless lives, including our own, are at stake. Our livelihoods also would stand a better chance at success if we'd just be still. It is not stagnant stillness, but stillness where we wait to hear from our creator and our inner selves.

(I rose to my feet when I was close to defeat.)

When I was close to defeat, this stillness helped me to rise to my feet. Being still and looking to my Maker sets me on a righteous course daily. A course that I couldn't adhere to while I was only trying constantly to demoralize myself. I remember being high enough to do the mundane and the more important tasks in everyday life. From going to 6 Flags to taking care of my babies. High at the family reunion and high at a relative's or friend's graduation kept me from my own graduation. Well, until now, anyway. I say that because this past Thursday, July 13, I, Obataiye, a.k.a. Will graduated from high school here at the Mountain View School. Lol, but on a serious note, y'all, the ceremony is this upcoming October. I'm geeked up, too. To my Caucasian brothers and sisters, geeked up is a good thing in this context. For the last seven years, I've been enrolled in school through all my ups and downs. To earn my high school diploma is surreal because of how far off course I was. They have a diploma program here in which we can take the GED test or whatever subject we choose. The program is based on the same credits we earned in our respective public schools. The school here sends for our records, and once they arrive here, our curriculum is situated. In the GED section, I scored 162, which my teacher had me geeked up when he told me 162 was a college-bound type of score. I feel so good. I have to speak on it.

When I was expected to stay in the thug box, I saw more. I chose to enroll in school for daily classes as opposed to just testing out. I craved what I'd often reminisced about: my school days. I was raised by Ms. Marzie Hattie Morgan, and those who know my beloved grandma know she meant business. May she rest better now. Gram was an elementary school teacher and taught middle school, too, at some point. The incomparable Marzie Morgan hails from Pittsburgh Hill District, where she taught at Miller. She also spent many of her precious years at

Northview Elementary. She taught at Allegheny Middle School also. I'm talking about all hood schools. But let's talk about outside the box. Gram also tended the bar at Mevius Cornfield on Webster Ave before it was the V.I.P. Uncle Melvin was like a brother to my gram and paid her well. Now, my grandmother did her fair share of sippin' back then, but her priority was her family and first grandson, yours truly. She didn't play any games about her Oball. So much so that she'd have me brought to her bar to see me and spend time with her Pooh. Pooh was the nickname that she called me in my earliest years.

I'd be in the Cornfield getting loved on by gram, Uncle Melvin, DOC, and many others who knew and loved my gram. I'd 5O-cent piece and quartered up leaving out of there. My first time in a bar was at the Cornfield at two years old.

And I was the youngest patron also. A lot of my coins were spent in little vending machines that spit out five and a half cashew pieces or gumballs, or even Mike & Ikes. I couldn't get enough of that junk food and the pork skins behind the bar. I was all outside the box. I was being raised in a Muslim household by Muslim parents; however, I was also spending money at the bar and drinking wine. If that's not outside the box, I don't know what is. What can I say? I've never liked boxes, and even if my name was Jack, I still couldn't do the box thing. I just don't fit in anybody's box. Even the big ole pleasure box: womanizing, hedonism, red eye sin, not realizing the lies embedded in all that pleasure. The devil is a liar. The pleasure is the subterfuge in the upper drawers of his tool chest. Is it really a wonder-type deal, laying with a trick, tricking, turning a trick, as they say? Then turn up broke, robbed in an alley, or in an ICU with full-blown AIDS. Or how about how we like to trap, although circumstances have called for survival to be activated? Once we're trapped in the trap with a music device full of trap music, it even gets searched and seized, too, if it has any residue.

Then, all the good sense we have starts to come to the surface. Not all the time, but many times over and over again, brothers and sisters, young and old, do finally get it.

A lot of the music artists, actors, athletes, and even teachers of different sorts that we admire have taken their lumps early or late and left for the hills. Beverley Hills, that is. Finally, exiting the mediocrity box of repeated mistakes or stupid choices cloned and bounced off the walls of the box. The bouncing idiot balls just batter and bruise our lives unnecessarily. How long and what will it take to get us to do better by our young, by ourselves, and by our Maker, who generously gives His sustenance and subsistence to all His children? Chances do run out at some point. They almost ran out in my life, but I'm coming up out of hate. This is too much like a box, and you already know how I feel about folks' boxes and whatnot. It's not that much getting high or just acting crazy in the world that's worth losing our freedom—especially our soul. To gain the world and lose the soul is something to ponder.

Now, I'm thinking of gaining full influence over my soul, though, and gaining the world. This is a better proposition, sistren and brethren, young and old. To be a soul controller of our own soul is to transcend all their boxes, including the jails. So many beautiful human beings are wasting away in and out of these prisons.

As a youngin, my little sister Marzie's dad, Harry, used to say us kids had no discipline. Being the oldest of my siblings, I had a chip on my shoulders, especially because I've always known and loved my biological pops. Truth be told, though, all Harry was saying was that there was a need for proper guidance. He understood that proper guidance ultimately leads to kids attaining self-awareness, eventually leading to self-mastery. The deeper one plummets into the depths of hedonism, the harder it is to regain proper footing on life's trials. Look at where

I'm at and consider what I must say. I was always hitting the streets, getting chemicaled up, and having false fun in front of my thoughts.

I can remember being in high school, schooling to be exact. All that a group of us wanted to do was smoke weed outside the school and smoke cigarettes in the bathrooms. The kids who were there to learn resented us. Hence the term, group.

They were from a foreign group, and normal kids and students quickly escaped our description. My group mostly consists of those in the jails or worse. The normal group couldn't even use a normal, healthy bathroom. As sure as my name is Obataiye, most times, it was like dark storm clouds in the restrooms. The kids that would make eye contact with us would say, "How stupid could you possibly be?" "You are who my parents warned me about." I acted cool with it, but privately, I always tuned into what normal people think about my hooliganism. Quite frankly, it bothered me because, inherently, I knew I was better than how I was behaving. We thought we owned the bathrooms. Even in class, I'd anticipate getting out of the books and into the bathroom stalls. I met another supposed-to-be student we'll call "T" in the bathroom. We recognized each other from my neighborhood in the Hill District. He wasn't from the Hill, but his girlfriend was. We always crossed each other's paths in the neighborhood and then at school.

In true form, we started a conversation in the bathroom over stinky cigarettes and out came a little brown jar. I had what was called a rush back then. It was a liquid legally sold under the name "rush" in most "head" shops throughout Pittsburgh. They cost 2 or 3 bucks if I didn't scorch up my memory whiffing the chemical concoction. I'd whiffed it before on my own, as it was a known drug amongst the young hedonists. Before you know it, "T" and I always broke out these little brown bottles, whiffing or huffing in school. The headrush lasted for 20 to 30 seconds. It really amazed us to be dizzy like this. Thinking back on this is sobering, ironically, but for lack of a better term.

It gets even more sobering, though, sistren and brethren. T ended up being one of three other cellmates I had at SCI-Cresson. Of course, the state pen was patiently waiting for us to use their bathrooms. Dropouts, to say the least. While we both still smoked cigarettes, the rush was nowhere to be found. These were drugs in the jail, but we were both trying to get out of prison. It was actually an honor block we were on, hence the two other cellmates. However, if we were honorable, we would've stayed in class instead of the school bathrooms and made the honor roll. Then we wouldn't be in prison in the mountains in a cage with TVs called the honor block. Suffice it to say, we opted out of rolling with a rush or any other drug.

We both wanted very much to be freed from this mountain-top destination for dropouts who dropped into the school battle-rooms in a rush. "T" would end up getting his wish as he was released before me. Wouldn't you know that all that rush in our earlier days truly obviously fried his brain? "T" was back on Cresson Mountain with me within six months for snatching a purse and violating parole terms. His craving for harder drugs got the best of his efforts to stay free. I really do want to move on to the next chapter, "but wait, there's more."

Now, I'm next up to bat at freedom park as my release date arrives in 2003. As I approached the park, I felt trepidation, as I was rusty at everything about being free. However, I towered over home plate, eager to swing for my first home. This pitcher I faced was no rookie and had an innumerable strike-out record. Everybody calls him the "strike-out kid," but his real name is patience.

Patience and I had faced off many times before 2003, and I was thinking, *I've got you right where i want you.* Patience wound up and threw a heater - I locked onto it and swung with everything. Suddenly, the park instantly darkened on me, and when I came, I was in the same mountains again. This time, I hit it out of the park alright, but the "it" was me, and now I was in the West Virginia Mountains.

It is not the resort but the ones adjacent to Cresson Mountain SCI. This nightmarish blackout sprung me forth a little better than two months ahead. I beat "T's" record of 6 months played repeatedly in my mind.

When I came to, l had accumulated several thousand dollars, so I was able to bail out at that time. I promptly called my children's mother and sister and instructed them to grab some money from my stash. I politicked on the inside and procured a bondman's number who would ultimately be persuaded by the lady power in my corner to free me. He was hesitant as I was from out of state. He couldn't resist, though, because my children's mother was a very beautiful white young lady - my third caddy, she, and my sister pulled up and was white too. I guess this bondsman said hold up - upon rethinking this - this guy has it all figured out, so I'll give him a shot. Lo and behold, my name was called the next day after my arrival at that facility in the woods, and before you knew it, I was rolling up the route to connect with 79 North back to the Steel City.

Again, I really do want to move on to this next chapter because it's relevant and good, but wait - you guessed it - there's more.

Now, I'm out on bond from the Great Mountain State, which I consider my third home. Fayette County was my first. I surely wasn't trying to go back to west V to face this drug charge. As small as it was, I still would rather West V not be my third home at that particular time.

Even the truest hedonist gets tired of the mountains at a certain point, especially when there are bars involved. That doesn't include liquor unless its squeezed oranges gathered from block mates and fermented bread that was barely spared due to hunger pains and no commissary. Would you believe that even after all the disdain I have for prison-issued outfits, hallways, dorms, cells, and bails within that same year of 2003, I'd be locked up again? (Greensburg, then Rockview with T yet again) Yup, right back at it. As a God-fearing man, I know He didn't cause all these trials; however, He surely chastised me.

Through every tribulation period, He's been right there with me. The fiery trials are where He demonstrates His saving power. Just like He did for Shadrach, Meshack, and Abednego. Jesus was right there in the flames with these three journeymen. When they emerged from the fire, the authorities and everyone who gathered around and observed were astonished. Not only were they shocked at these men's unaffected bodies, but the smell of fire couldn't be detected. It didn't exist. With all this flame chasing I did, brethren and sistren, I'd sure need my Maker's extinguishing grace before long. Without doubt or fail, He showed up and showed me the way out of the fiery steel bars of prison again in early 2006. I was extradited back to West V after the PA Supreme Court affirmed the lower court decision to suppress all evidence against me. I had sat for 3 1/2 years in Greensburg, PA, county jail, hearing from the Holy Spirit the whole time. Just before I was extradited to West V to face the charges, I skipped bail. He showed me the most shocking vision ever. I never uttered a word about it to anyone, although I should have. Before I knew it, I was whisked to the Northern Regional jail in Doddridge County West V. I'd hoped and prayed the transporting officers would never arrive, meaning the case would be dropped. That prayer wasn't answered. At least not like I'd imagined it would be. God works in mysterious ways, but He works.

After sitting in the regional facility for four months, thinking the worst, I finally got called for a court hearing. This was truly out of the blue. I still remember how nice it was that day. The West Virginian sky was a clear blue hue of perfection. Seven of us were handcuffed and shackled to each other and ordered out to the van. We all took 3-inch steps and slid out the door. The sky seemed to just open up and say hi to us with the bling of the radiant sun that was on full display. Silently, I hoped and prayed that I could be free again to enjoy a day just like the one we beheld while cuffed and shackled. They say the sky's the limit, but all we could do was look because we were booked. We were limited to 3-inch steps and slides across our capture's seemingly secret parking lot. As we boarded the van, all of our eyes lit up. Just to be riding seemed to be freeing in itself. Surely, we all reminisced silently about better days under similar skies. And now, all for the sake of our hedonistic ways, we had to endure a little, some a lot more, to get to and through the great door (go back into the dream you had about Breal).

On this amazing, awe-inspiring day, things would continue to get better and better. I intuitively felt this humongous optimism despite my cuffed and shackled disposition. We traveled about fifteen miles from Dodridge to Clarksburg West V. We dropped off a guy and picked one up. Then, on to Fairmont, WV, my stomach was tied in knots. I kept imagining the best and worst outcomes almost simultaneously. It was really nerve-racking. As we entered the small town bullpen facility, I smelled freedom. It was almost informal and casual. The entrance led into the very small receiving room that reminded me of the mom & pop store in the hill district. I almost thought I could just ask to be let out the door. The officers were constables of African descent weighing 350 pounds or better, reminding me of uncle and cousin, so and so. Even the white officer was super laid back and just there for his check. They led us to a little cell slash double room that was divided in two by a drop ceiling and card board walling.

They split us up, three on one side and the rest on the other. There were mounted color TVs in each little cell with rap city on both of them. I couldn't believe it. This was too strange. It really felt almost dreamy and surreal. We were handed lunch bags with sandwiches, chips, and a juice box. The videos blared as I ate and I vividly saw myself free-riding in my new whip, listening to what I was watching.

The next thing I knew, my name was called within an hour to go out and speak to my court-appointed lawyer. He was cool on the other side of the pillow as he said I might be leaving today. I almost exploded in surges of great emotion and exuberance. I very much wanted to be free from the cuffs and bars that halted my movement. We were called into the adjoining courtroom within fifteen minutes after seeing my attorney. Three and a half years, almost four years, had passed since I'd bonded out from that drug case. There was no physical evidence of the conspiracy to make a drug sale case. The C.I. that was allegedly sent to buy drugs evidently smoked up the evidence. The case was a waste of taxpayers' money, especially to extradite me to WV and to house and feed me. Suffice it to say the Good Lord works in mysterious but sure ways. I was given time served, to which I gladly pleaded. The judge asked If I wanted to address the courts, and I said, "Your honor, I just want to go home and start a new life with my babies. I'll never come to WV again with ill intent." He obliged and warned me to do just that, but he did it politely and kindly. I almost ran out of the courtroom through the shackles and cuffs. Within a few hours of that plea deal, I was once again a free man.

My whole being was animated with enthusiasm as a kid at Disneyland. I was released at the same time as another guy from the regional jail back in Doddridge County. We were very deep in the woods, too. No one knew I was being released in my family, so a ride was in lieu. I have no fear, though, as this continuous wave of good vibes still flows through my way.

I got my money at the front desk and began making phone calls in the lobby. The other guy who was released did the same on the other phone. My contacts were minimal, but I put out the SOS that I needed to be rescued from those woods ASAP. The lady behind the counter informed me and the other guy that a C.O. would be on his way out momentarily and might possibly give us a ride into Clarksburg. He was going on official jail business, and sure enough, he let us hitch a ride with him in the big ole van again, except this time, there were no shackles and cuffs involved. Once in Clarksburg, we got out near an Open Pantry Store. The other releasee was a native Clarksburgian and said his mom might take me the hour and a half into Pittsburgh.

On the way to his house, four partiers were lying back on their porch. Phones outside with their cigarettes, too. As we strolled by, I politely asked to use their phone and told them I was fresh out of jail. They offered me a cigarette and let me call until my heart was content. It was a good thing because the guy I got released with walked into his house four doors up, came back out in three seconds, and said his mom couldn't do it. I said to myself, "Yeah, right, but it didn't matter as I almost made myself at home on Nola's porch. Nola was the owner of the phone and renter of the porch, and I was now a piece of furniture on it.

I wasn't budging until I got a hold of somebody to come the short distance to get me. I finally contacted my lil brothers, Jibreel and young Jim. They were both geeked up to hear from me and jumped right on the highway. They were there in no time to get big bro. Not only were the lanes they rode in to get me fast lanes, but Clarksburg was a fast one-lane all three of us knew too well. This made them even more eager to come pick me up there, especially when I told them ahead of time that I was on the porch of some real groovy West Virginians who liked to partake in all of our hedonistic ways. In no time flat, I was being picked up physically and mentally.

When my lil bros got to Clarksburg, I felt like a rocket lifting off. I hadn't seen Jibreel or young Jim in for a while. I introduced them both to everyone on the porch; phone numbers were exchanged, and we were on our way. On the way to Pittsburg, it felt surreal to be in the presence of these young kings. My beloved lil brothers, whom I watched grow into fathers, were just trying to see some true daylight in life, just like I was. All three of us ate together on more than one occasion in pursuit of a full belly and a full life over the years. Suddenly, after hitting the blunt of high-quality marijuana, they passed me a darkness closed in on me. It was the dream I had back in Westmoreland County Jail. I dreamed Jibreel got shot several times before I woke up sweating and upset. I kept it to myself as if to just stuff it into nonexistence.

When we touched down off interstate 79, moving through those Fort Pitt tunnels, all I could think of was the three letters W.0.W.! To see those three rivers merge once again and the glisten and mighty ripple in the waves, with the fountain roaring like I remembered at Point State Park was a dream manifestation at its finest.

Our first stop was "G" block, named after Jibreel and young Jim's very close friend and comrade, aka "Gute." Hence the term "On Gute you crazy like." Elmore Square was the original name of the housing project. That all changed in the mid to late 90s when young Gute got killed. May he rest in peace. So many more of my young brothers from Elmore and all over the Hill District would meet their fate smack dab in the middle of Hedonist highway. Massive guns made up the traffic on this highway. It's not your average highway. In fact, the turnout was low, although we all stayed high, striving to find ways and means to do what we knew and what we observed in our environments. This often meant that, in one perception, there were winners and losers, but a more accurate truth was all loose on the low way. That's why it's imperative that we all - as many that will - heed their higher selves yet in the victory lane and out of the box. That box life often leads to off life the hard way.

On drugs, stressed out in a rut. The ultimate though is dead - backdoored by somebody that said "love you bro" two days before he smoked you like the weed y'all was pulling on. That's the time for a new box that gets lowered into the ground surrounded by loved ones in agony. I know about this all too well.

Fast forward to the film of this true story. Not too far, though, because ten months later, I was released from West V's prison system yet again. This time, with two murder charges and two attempted murder charges, minus my baby brother. I was facing myself in all actuality - in another box where all four panels were the effect and sum total of the cause of hedonism at the end of the day. This time, it ended my baby brother's days on earth and my freedom. Talk about a rough spot. In and out of those boxes and subsequent rough spots puts folks out of commission. For all those reading these words with similar experiences, please never lose faith in what's right. God's path is right, so move with intelligence through all the rough spots and pray no matter what or how low you feel.

THE PRIDE BOX

As we continue to unpack these boxes, there's no way we forget this one. It's a big one, too. One of the biggest, I must say myself. It's none other than the pride box that is responsible for more than just heartache. It's known for stopping the beating of our beloved muscle of life. Now, this box is worthy to be very weary of, for it is stealthy, crafty, and artful. It is not the beautified art, but the stealthiness contained in its chambers will definitely bomb your life and others partly because it can and often does reside inside of us all. Can there be a more befitting time than this to talk and shine light into this dark box? The light will surely obliterate it, although, like the Terminator movie, it reforms again and again and again.

This is a hell of a box! It's listed in The Bible as one of the seven deadliest sins for a reason. Pride pulls up on us when we're kids, knowing it will be nurtured and told how cute it is. Before you know it, kabooooooom temper, tantrums, cussing folks out, wanting to dress like adults, the makeup at, and so on. It all ties into pride early because we really don't recognize it as harmful. To be dignified and loved healthily is one thing, but if we're not careful, we get angry bundles of pride with legs and arms that kick and punch, not the bundles of joy expected at first. This is raw but real and partly to blame for the unrest of our civilization.

Using myself as the exemplar of our subject, I say to my on-lookers, "Look at me now." Ever since I can remember, I was told how cute I was, how curly my hair was, and how nice my name was. My parents instilled in me that my name meant King of The World, which it does. I love them for that; however, I was never taught humility. To their credit, they were both very young at my birth, so they gave me what they knew and what they could. This is for us, the later generations, to be very mindful of. A lot of this explosiveness being expressed in shootouts and fights at every gathering is the effect of pride. It didn't just appear out of thin air. Of course, there are other causes of the madness of today, but let's address this one, which we can rid ourselves of. I mean, we can go into the slavery thing, oppression, and racism, but I figure we remedy all that by winning in spite of it all.

One sure way to win is to master ourselves and help our babies learn healthy ways to do the same early on. We've all heard the phrase, 'it starts at home.' Well, whether we want to admit it or not, that's true. These boxes addressed here don't have to be addressed to us anymore. I'm tired of losing out on the best in life and settling for a hot car, a chain, some shoe box money, and no house or generational wealth. Not having a conscious connection to the Most High is even more than all that. I put myself as the most high without really knowing it. "I'm the king of the world." I'm the king of the world because my mom and dad told me so, and my name means king of the world. Mom and Dad didn't know I would take that and really toy running the world. I'm sure, but that's what I did. I was more loving than Hitler, though. He was missing God in his whole approach. I've always acknowledged God because mom, dad, and grandma definitely taught me who my creator was. And for that, I am forever grateful because my spirituality and God have been my anchor. The storms that come with pride never fail to churn up some rough waters. The only true anchor is our Creator. The street life and drug game seemed to be the answer, but when I looked deeper, I was sitting in this closet with a window, and an crimanally and monetarily overcharged $5,000 18-inch TV. I'm not defined by any boxes or mistakes, and this TV is only 50 bucks out there in the world. Here, they want both arms and legs. If this is what pride brings, I'm giving it back, brethren and sistren. It's just not worth my peace of mind, body, and spirit. We weren't made for this type of existence. Don't get me wrong, because many live and dwell in prison out there, too. But of the mental type of prison where the bars are just as real as the ones I look through. Anytime we choose to continually put our lives and freedom on the line, it's suspect. I thought I needed to put it all on the line. I told myself and others that hustling and street life were all I knew.

I was lying to myself, and deep down inside, I knew it. That was just that box life getting at me and winning. I was losing, and inherently, I knew it, but again, pride welled up, and the facade went up around it. If pride has a shell, its name is facade. After years of beating myself up with those peanuts, A.K.A. money, it had gotten so real. To the point where I would be crying, leaving out to go and risk it all. My son Jamil saw me crying as I left and said, "Mommy, why is daddy crying?" Then he asked me, and it stopped me in my tracks. I shut the door· and came back and picked my baby boy up. I held him close as he wiped my eyes, and I said, "Daddy got to go get that cash." The pride inside me told me I was keeping it real and gangster. The truth in me pushed out more tears because I knew I could do better for my loved ones, myself, and my God. Jamil's mother, Melissa, wiped my eyes as all three of us hugged, and she softly told me, "Baby, why don't you just quit? You know you don't have to keep doing this, and I'm not with you for the money. We can get jobs and just have each other and raise our kids." Pride box said, "She's lying, Ob, you need to be rich right now and can be, so go do you." I promised her and Jamil I'd be back and that I'd stop hustling very soon, but very soon came, and I got locked up within weeks.

Mellissa was pregnant with my daughter, whom we named Endure. Lord knows even she had to endure the struggle of the stress I put her mother through. Yes, even in the womb, she received the vibes of the effects of the pride her dad was dealing with. Those boxes do this when we don't explore them with rays of light from inside and above. I was feeding the box, buying cars and rings and things. I felt like a king, alright. I didn't own one castle or house, for that matter. I looked like a trillion, but surely the devil is a lie, and deep inside, that's how I felt. Something just didn't feel right; day after day and night after night, a sense of doom haunts me.

In that jail cell, I still didn't realize the doom I previously sensed was manifesting. It was obvious to one who is truly paying attention to life and it's unfolding, not just here for the ride. Had I been really paying attention, that jail trip would've been my last one. My enemy in-me was saying, "Man, you're a living legend, Obataiye. It doesn't stop with a little shake-up like this. You gotta eat, dawg." And those kids deserve the world." Head in the clouds - looking all buff, feeling like I owned the world but not a house. In all this thinking I was doing, I forgot that I had recommitted my life to Christ during this time. In essence, I forgot Jesus is the king, for real.... Now, in all this forgetting, I was resolved to get rich and get out before anything terrible happened.

Upon my release and in no time flat, no stopwatch could record the time of how fast I had a package in my hands. These are just a few dangers that come with this pride thing. I'm sure you know what I mean. My intentions were good but not good enough because when good actions don't follow good intentions, bad things happen. Kids grow up fatherless, and their mothers suffer too, although given enough jail, they'll move on. Some quicker than others. I got so humble when my lady would show signs of pulling away. You know it when it starts. It's always a process. First, she stopped answering on the first or second ring like she used to. Then comes the stuttering and how the phone was acting up. Then came the arguments about what I was doing when I was out there and who I was doing it with. Mind you, this was acceptable or at least tolerated when I was out there providing. Now there's a next up, and the phone just breaks finally…. We all know ain't that much phone breaking in the world. One thing that broke, though, was my heart and that pride inside that had me blinded by the bling of those rings I had on. I could see real good now. I could also feel the unyielding pain that I allowed to enter the job market or indulge my entrepreneurial spirit on the legal side. I forfeited a very precious jewel. Not my rings and chains but my freedom yet again.

This room I'm in is surely another box, but the difference is my mind is free. Now I realize that my goals have always been normal, healthy goals. It's just that my ways and means sent forth goalies that fought me tooth and nail so that I wouldn't score. There's no question whether the criteria I applied to my movement were coherent. It obviously wasn't due to the tight squeeze of the box life. With peace of mind and clarity of thought, we realize and exhilarate. Despite my placement, I'm learning afresh each day and bringing into play my previously unused capabilities. Getting to know myself, I've become in tune with true power. It's called decisions and choices, and it is made from a mental space of healthy determination. I refused to be tagged as overly and blindly ambitious and being tricked into believing that all I know is drug sales. With those sales come guns eventually.

Studying, reading, learning, and praying were game changers for me, and stopping my mental reign was not in the forecast. I've lost a lot over the years due to living in boxes. Some were more comfortable than others, but I thank God that none could hold me back. We are all blessed with mental agility, but we first have to stop, look, and listen. In that stillness, we catch our breath, recalibrate, and clearly see what results we've incurred thus far. Ponder this: Pride calls for us to hold onto certain lofty, haughty aspects of our old lifestyle. Our higher self calls for us to allow for the dismantling of the false mantle. Once analysis is made, decisions are enriched with good sense. Lift off, leaving all boxes in oblivion to turn to dust. Truly, sistren and brethren, knowledge is transformational when we use it. To have it and not use it is actually shameful.

For most of us, there are no excuses to continue to fail after the first few times or so. It gets old after a while, and we can't keep saying we slipped into the box. At a certain stage, it's, "No, you walked into the box; now, deal with it." Granted, in the hood and nowadays in the world, the atmospheric pressure is tremendous. The remedy that I highly advise is to humble down and pray. Humility is opposite to pride, and it creates harmony, and harmony begets happiness. We deserve to be happy after going through so much. Now, it's time to do even more than survive. Surviving is the primary and mediocre frame of reference. It's about overcoming and commandeering our lives. High-level activism leaving the dope knowing hope is the antidote. We begin to put real effort into family cohesion and coherence. We need to get in tune with who we are when sober-minded and poised. We must begin to form new positive circles of like-minded friends and associates. In this new, fresh thinking process, the Most High uses the universe to deliver the perfect tools, books, jobs, and legal connections in perfect timing. Collaborative efforts are needed to ensure success is conceived and birthed.

As business owners, positive thinkers, and high-level athletes, we capture old and new opportunities in life's great arena. This new trajectory of thought culminates in victory after victory. You think the box throwers were hating before. Well, that hate continues and, in some cases, even intensifies. (The only boxes I get into these days are elevators) King Obataiye went into exile, and I offer no excuse, but there's none. No weapons formed against me will prosper, not even those in my own flesh. What He started, He'll finish. However, we're well equipped now with the armor of God as we care for these babies and our nation as a whole. So that big ole hate box only serves as fuel to these power thrusters. With new, fresh, and blessed ideas, elevators are the only boxes we get into these days. All those subliminal hate speeches and inauthenticity acid a nitro effect to the thrusters.

Obataiye went into exile, admittedly, and 1 offer no excuses, but there are none. My Lord and Savior Jesus Christ said that what He starts, He also finishes, and He brought me out still a King. Call me Obataiye, but never the guy in the box.

THE PEOPLE PLEASER BOX

After kicking all these boxes out of the way, we travel - this one is no exception. This one is shifty and sometimes deep-laid, so we must be more insightful. Yes, insightful because its conception comes from within us. Even so, when others see a reminisce of it, they'll try to exploit it.

Allowing this box to exist means inviting the machinations of many who pose as friends. In reality, it's hard to resist utilizing the levers that people pleasers expose.

For anyone, being a decent person doesn't entail being a doormat. So, dismantling the levers and this box is a must-do right now. You don't have to live in this box even if your name is Jack. In addition to Dapper ole head, who taught Dave and me the lesson on perseverance, another brain session stated that folks will play you how you play yourself. In other words, the way we present to anyone, friends, family, or foe is their read and leads to how they treat us.

Going into beatboxing and rapping approval, I received it, and my generation as a whole was very pleased with each other. This was key in how I became addicted to always seeking folks' approval through their admonition. Although the initial teaching I received was verbal, the adversities of forgetting it were heartfelt.

Remembering our lessons in life is huge because the stakes are so high. Just look around you; whether on the news or the people around you, the realities of mental illness, drug abuse, and anti-social folks are raw and real. Most, if not all, of these beautiful people were normal, healthy, and optimistic at one point. Somewhere on their journey, they were sidetracked. Their suffering can't be downplayed or negated because it weighed on their inner scale of peace of mind. Agree with it or not, hurt people, hurt people. Unhealthy habits, ideas, and attitudes like always seeking folks' approval or trying too hard to please can have dramatic and dire results. These are very real experiences of our nation's babies and ourselves, to be blunt - when we're not careful. The consequences may vary and often do.

Anxiety is a big one that ensues when one feels exponentially concerned with seeking folks' approval (not approval to do a certain thing but a sort of telepathic approval likened to fake love or false admiration). Incessantly crying about how the real Jack feels about what you do presents you as a potential mini-Jack. Flunky, offer this, then that; when you get back, it is just a bunch of Jack.

These are extreme parts of the spectrum, but they are insidious and very true. As a young beatboxer and rapper, I received massive approval and admiration. This was exhilarating and encouraging as it was for all the other partakers of the arts. One difference with me was that due to the adversity of childhood molestation, I needed all that cheering and rooting I received when I took center stage or center sidewalk, shall I say.

The battles and the shows took place on sight when our crew would encounter each other. I loved every minute of it, too. My beats let the onlookers and listeners tell it was top-rated at any and every event. They let me know about it, too. Almost every day, wherever I was, I'd be asked to hit the blu tu glu beat. This beat was one honed with my big brother Doug Braxton up on Webster Ave and Wandless. It was and still is a very different beat from any most have heard. My crew - The G.P.C., aka The Get Paid Crew, would get the lion's share of the household Hill District born beat. It was all amazing all the time, and at 51 years old, someone would remind me of something I hadn't seen for 35 years. "Ob, hit the blu tu glu tune." I just cracked up laughing. Who doesn't love to be loved? Especially when it's real. And that's just it. I was practically pampered with all that love as a youngin, and to think it was waning devastated me at times when the super-thug era took full swing. I felt rich with no money because I was in non-tangibles. The subsiding of the love or approval waves, real or imagined, shocked and shook me up undeniably.

As we got older, things got more real. Robberies and much more occurred in the trenches, and cracks in the concrete left by the heavy blows of the devil's poop. Cookies was the nickname for the rocks that were being thrown at these jails. Little did we know there's a stark difference between this aftertaste and the one left by oreos and milk. From where I sit, the applicable similarity is this and the ice-cold milk that the cookies were dipped into. Even before the jailhouse, to be precise. In the cold, we sometimes find ourselves in one of these boxes, whether Jack is the name or not. We can wound up looking for that approval we enjoyed as youngins. If not in one way, the other may pertain depending on one's proclivities, advantages, or disadvantages. It stems from the distant past, which we all need to let go of. Holding on to even the past triumphs can prove very painful or fatalistic. This box can smother you straight out.

Sometimes, we've hurt so many people in the low-lying trenches that when we start to rise a bit, we seek to be overly apologetic, even to folks we didn't hurt. Paradoxically, there's honor in this box, but the fact that it's a box is the downside. We've already been down long enough, brethren and sistren. The Most High made us to be up and hold on to his love. Not beholden to the ghost of the past. So, dishonor comes when we play like we are less than any man or woman. Indeed, we are more than conquerors in Jesus; in Him, no weapons formed against us shall prosper, including these harmful boxes.

Admittedly, the pressure mounts as all four sides of the box press in. However, we are privileged to take on a more precious form than any ordinary jewel. And we thought all it did was bust pipes and make diamonds. The only expectations we honor are our Maker's and those who authentically root for us.

There's no reasonable time to invest in trying not to deviate from box throwers' expectations.

Any other movement that doesn't illuminate our path forward in its expression must be repression, which inevitably leads to depression. There is no future in going crazy trying to please the unpleasable. All this madness is often at the expense of our needs.

We need our babies to be healthy, safe, and successful. We need our families by our side and at their annual reunions with all involved loving on each other. We need our real friends to know we reciprocate their love and concern for us. These are true needs. No cigarettes, pills, and personal stashes of blow that await the stressed out and unhappy. I said unhappy because that is the sum of such a sad reality. Conundrum is an understatement for the state of mind in the whirlwind of self-destruction. To bring this profound insanity to a halt is to recalibrate and lift off. When we start to dream again, as opposed to having nightmares or no sleep at all, it is to live again. Being boxed up with deep feelings of guilt and shame because we don't fit the bill is a non-starter.

There will be no lift-off without the start of the transcendence engine. Two super inspirational examples of transcendence are: when the founders of our great nation decided on independence. Another powerful one is when the spirit of freedom moved in our forefathers, culminating in freedom for African Americans. Surely the list of these two off the top of my head shouldn't be taken for granted or overlooked as a given. This big dance we're privy to is way bigger than any superbowl. This is the big dance of life and freedom, and we forfeit the game and dignity when we constantly seek the approval of others.

The right folks will be drawn to us automatically, and we will be drawn to them. When we think right, we do right, and right comes. When a lot of what we do is right, the forcefield of love abounds and repels the wrong. In so doing, we revel in the joy of our decisions. What we end up with tomorrow is predicated upon what we decide today and now. "Do I chase the crowd knowing more than half of them don't like me because I'm me? Or do I open this book on real estate, investing, or maybe even stay in and be with my kids?

The power is in the choice, you know? Corrosion of our best qualities = implosion, resulting in the walking dead. The other choice is to allow hope to explode and rain down substances that will revitalize our aspirations to action. Let's face it - losing is an option, but it's just not viable. The world can be cold, right? But it can also warm up like this past summer. The rising of the heat did a sweep - keyword rising. Some even called it the summer of Co Co. I couldn't help but catch Co Co's vibe when she found that special reserve gear, slightly tilted her head down but not to mope. She was locking in to win y'all. She intently focused, kept her composure, aimed for the sky, and that engine roared and flamed into lift-off. What could be more perfect? This young lady warrior scorched the court with a heat that she proclaimed was aided by the gas poured onto her flame by who else than those all so famous haters and nay-sayers. The ones we tried to please and get them to approve of us.

Take a page from Co Co's book, and let's get a summer or two named after us. We are definitely in the greatest arena known to humanity. It's called life, and it's a great privilege under the pressures that come with it. However, no pressure, no diamond, right? Brethren and sistren, if there ever was a time to make an observation, it's now. Most people we try to please and those whose approval we seek are betting in the back rooms that we lose. The stakes are too high for us to miss this. All of our real friends and loved ones are rooting for us, even if and when we don't know they are. Life in shambles doesn't matter because real love is unconditional and has no flip side. Those who truly admire us root for us even when our fortune takes a downward spiral.

The naysayers forget or just don't know that after the storm's spiral comes, the sun shines and the upward shift of The Godly wind. What they also forget is the devil is a lie. That dude came to steal, kill, and destroy, but Christ came so that we might have life and have it more abundantly than ever before. My brothers and sisters of whatever ethnicity, gang, state, or neighborhood. Please know that our true strength is in our connection and oneness with God - not nobody's box. It's time to commandeer our lives back and remember that right thinking precedes right actions, and right actions beget a good life. Real life outside the box is the only way to live, and love, respect, and honor are the best things to give.

We first have to give those to ourselves, which doesn't entail being boxed up for anyone or currying and scurrying for their favor. We are favored by the most powerful force in the universe, beloved. And that's the biggest fact that exists. We need to be ever mindful of who we are and who we were and are meant to be. Even if we flunked in school, flunky is not who we are. In addition, when we shoot, we're shooting for the stars and not each other. Keep in mind a gun is not always needed to shoot a brother or sister down. When we try to enclose folks off in boxes of disdain of any sort, the box is reopened. To help someone get up is to help yourself.

Ponder the fact that we get what we put out into the universe. To all my kin, not necessarily by skin. Remember to set boundaries starting today. Recognize any tendency in yourself to subordinate your goals, dreams, and immediate peace of mind just to superficially please others. There's an uneasiness that comes with the futility of pleasing people. This disease is an indicator of wrong direction in our thinking. This built-in hazard signal is analogous to those in the newer vehicles.

When swerving into a potentially dangerous object, an alert sounds off. The same thing occurs with us and in us. We are made in the image of The Most High, not the most low. It's time to realize this truth; get up and go. In fact, we often tend to go ·with the tide or the wave, as they say. Our inner selves, on the other hand, aren't culturally inclined. Once we introspectively peer back into ourselves instead of following our peers, we'll ignite that God-given light that we surely possess. There is a very stubborn reluctance to do what's best for us while we're so caught up in muck and mire. In times such as this, we tap into the athletic creativity we all have and might not know.

If you've ever endured and persevered through hard times, there's that athlete in life's great arena. So we see the muck and mire for what it is - hurdles - and then we dig deep and leap. In this mental state, as opposed to the subservience of the lower plane, we begin to see and realize the premium opportunities within our reach. Ponder, though, that premium opportunities require premium output. With this in mind, we couple it with our original selves. That dreamer before the dream killers approached. That confident - some's overconfident go-getter that surely still exists.

Now, in this great arena, sometimes there are losses to some extent. Take comfort in the fact that even in losses, there are wins. In the loss is agony, but as we agonize, we focus more on what we'd rather have and know we can attain. I could list many examples at this juncture of many who started out losing and found another gear. The gear that propelled them into success after success. I won't list any such folks, as this would be a perfect time to just reflect and embody that activism for yourselves. Those we listen to musically and watch so admiringly on the T.V. screen. Even many from the same trenches we trudged in. They hurt, they were abused, some went to jail and have been through hell then and now, but they tapped into that inner champion, and they prevailed.

When we tap into God-given willpower, we manifest hope, which is the antidote. One thing that works for me is glancing at the madness, the hate, the misconceptions, and the side eyes, which are all part of my frame of reference. Excellence fuel additives!! In fact, all those killjoys and perceived stumbling blocks turned out to be stepping stones. They were game changers for me. Admittedly, all those blindside hits and the ones I see coming surely hurt. Unyielding, I stand and move in the resurrection of Jesus Christ. Straight like that!!! The devil tried to tell me that I was weak and victimized. The Holy Spirit reminded me that I am strong, tenacious, and spiritualized. Brethren and Sistren, it's very important to self-reflect in the positive after those waves of negative feelings that come with the battles.

Yes, we were wounded, and the scars do exist, but the scars are sure testaments to our survival. The exit hole in the side of all those boxes proves who we really are. It's not what they say that counts; it's who we truly are that far exceeds their thought process. It's time to start honing in on our craft, talents, and careers. Maybe even enrolling in some schooling we may have missed or dropped out of. On July 13th, I finished high school. Finally, seven days later, I received my diploma, and next month, on October 17, 2023, I'll partake in the ceremony. It's been a haul, tug, and a push through it. It's also been exhilarating to activate parts of the brain that I hadn't used for years. That stagnation, stressing about all those imaginary monsters that are toothless up close, can actually cause atrophy. We must keep pushing through it all.

The naysayers will say this and that to deter us, but that's just part of the test before the testimony. Support systems will start to come into play for you as you move. Don't stay stuck, beloved. Study, learn, read, and build with your new positive circles. Some folks are doing what you want to do. The writers, the musicians, the painters, and the college students will gladly encourage you to join their ranks if you are sincere. Search your heart again instead of constantly searching for the needs of those who look down their noses at everyone except for those they tear. Thinking along the lines of any of these boxes is called distorted thinking. Tap into that clarity that awaits. Don't be afraid to go to the park by yourself. Pull out that fishing rod and relax.

Remember who you were before all the boxes and cast out your line. Look at that awesome reflection now looking back at you. There are ripples and waves, yet you still shine through them all. Now smile and pull your line back in. You'll be pleasantly surprised at your catch. We are duty-bound to be our best in this gift of life. We'd be derelict in our duty to fall off and stay off. Setbacks - they come - no doubt. But so do comebacks, beloved. Granted, many of us deal with the pain of those who seem to have departed from our side. Upon reflecting on this, you'll see that God never planned for certain people and us to stay in tune. In fact, they helped us tighten up. Keep this in mind, too, beloved. If they loved you and it turned into hate - the ladder was always true. Love doesn't die. It might not always be as pronounced and excited as in the beginning, but even after a fallout, the light fills the space where anger darkened. Maybe you feel beholden or like you owe your allegiance to those who harbor hate. The devil is a liar! We owe it to ourselves to earnestly live this gift, this present of the present time.

Every breath is a miracle and should be recognized as such; if not, something needs tuning and readjusting within ourselves. When we pay attention or define what we're dwelling on mentally, the causes lie in our external experiences. When I took that introspective view, I realized the immaturity of being needy of folks' approval. Sometimes, I wouldn't even feel good about life until I got that nod of approval from the big ugly box. Suffice to say, I x'd that box out. Maturity is necessary and starts when we turn the engine over and ignite the light. Has the journey been rough? Of course, it has, but we have grown in the rough. With major disruption comes major growth - that's if we're receptive to the substance behind it all.

The substance is The Most High's idea of the universe and nature. All the trees and flowers that yield us fruit, nectar, and honey for the bees had to endure the unthinkable. When they were yet seeds, they were stepped on, spat upon, poo-pooed on, urinated on, cold, dark, and lonely. On the same level as the worms and crawling things. Now look at them all around us. Whenever we walk, ride, or just look, eat, and become nourished by their sustenance, we discard the seeds. Now, we will have to go through these new ones to get it to all of you.

We can be our own besties or our own worst enemies. The choice is ours. Growth and high yield or stagnation and withering. It's time to let go of the old boxes for good. Treat ourselves to some nice shoes and even get rid of those boxes. No more boxes! We must leave the graveyard of disappointment and let down. We can't find new life in dead things. Approval by wrong thought is dead on arrival. There's nothing there. Nothing from nothing leads to nothing. We often unknowingly seek a state of mourning dealing with that approval box. Excuse me, but no excuses because we now know. The unused capabilities button has been located. There has been a successful culmination of everything we've endured and persevered through to get to this spaceship. Now push that button to ignite that light, use active vision goggles, and lift off. Look out the window at all those burning boxes now. Feel the exhilaration of marching the gas and not getting a speeding ticket. No speeding tickets in the sky. Let us pray and allow the waste gardener to water our individual seeds. We no longer allow external circumstances or people to thwart our growth. We are overcomers, and we overstand the circumstances and smash boxes while standing. The only use for an excuse is in the other meaning of the word when saying excuse while we lift off and take flight. Now tap and mash that will power pedal and go.

May peace and blessings be upon y'all.

About the Author

Obataiye Scott, born February 27, 1972, grew up in Pittsburgh, Pennsylvania for his entire life with the exception of a few years he spent in Los Angeles California, Carry North Carolina and Arlington Texas, with his Father and Step Mom. He's now 53 years experienced in life and learning and his fire still burns like it was day one.

In July of 2023 He graduated high school and received his diploma proving it's never too late to accomplish things. The following year he became a Certified Peer Specialist (See www.Paceboard.org #21349). For the past three years he's chaired AA and NA passionately with great appreciation. I'm a member of the Elsinore Bennu Think Tank for Restorative Justice out of Duquesne University and also a contributor of mind and experience to Voices for Juvenile Justice through my Brother Walter Harris. I am a writer and poet representing Christ first, the Family Unit Company/FAMMTREE.Life.